An Uncompromising Journey of a Contemporary Congregation

The Chronicle of a Pentecostal Congregational journey overcoming the unimaginable and unpredictable through uncompromising vision and uncharted collaborations.

A GUIDE FOR CHURCH PLANTING AND MINISTRY DEVELOPMENT

BISHOP SEDGWICK DANIELS

"It is a high honor for me to write the forward for this powerful book designed to assist leaders in maximizing their potential. I have personally witnessed the masterful leadership style of Bishop Sedgwick Daniels and I've gained many tools for successful ministry and best practices for business as a result of his tutelage. Bishop Sedgwick Daniels is a forward thinking quintessential leader who has his hand on the pulse of cutting edge 21st century ministry. He is a postmodern prophetic voice who delivers an ageless message, empowering men and women to effectively fulfill the great commission. This collection of wisdom filled nuggets is a direct reflection of Bishop Daniels powerful display of results driven ministry. He has a proven tract record of high success rates in leadership strategies and program development. The motivation and inspiration that readers will gain from this book will change the way they think and equip them with perspicacious concepts that will guarantee success if properly applied. The theological foundation built at the inception of this book provides a greater understanding as to why it is necessary to aim for excellence in ministry. In an age that is heavily influenced by social media and Hollywood fantasies, it is important for the church to remain centrally focused and rooted within our call to evangelize the world and empower men and women to embrace faith in Christ and disciple others. Having a vision is essential for successful ministry. Bishop Daniels explains the necessity of leaders not allowing their vision to be reduced to an undeveloped thought. Vision casting is urgent because the lack of vision can be lethal. This book will broaden the minds of its readers and will expose them to ways of expanding their capacity to serve their communities and congregations through partnerships and collaborations. Bishop Daniels has written this book to both speak to the tenured and the neophyte leader. Anyone who reads this book will have a greater knowledge of what is required to soar in whatever assignment God has given to their hands."

Superintendent Michiah J. Young, M. Div
Life Church of God In Christ

"We as believers fight daily against the deceptive tactics of the devil, tactics that involve oppression depression, violence and lack of identity. These issues plague many ministry leaders across the country which is why this book is a helpful tool to anyone that is currently involved in ministry or looking to start a ministry. Bishop Daniels empowers you as the reader to remain vigilant to the great commission of Christ. There is no denying that this book gives the reader the very blueprint on dismantling the tactics of the devil while building the kingdom of God in a real and practical way."

Elder Kevin Cooper, M.Div
Little Rock, Arkansas (Former Holy Redeemer Intern)

"Church leaders desire to cultivate innovative and creative leadership abilities as they navigate today's Christian society, and as their congregations anticipate spiritual insight and divine guidance. Bishop Sedgwick Daniels takes a fresh glimpse into this pertinent need, by drawing upon his experience as a master administrator, educator, and community leader. He then strategically incorporates them with spiritual practices found within the discipline of spiritual direction.

As a recipient of the masterful tutelage of Bishop Daniels, I can attest that the techniques of spiritual proclivity inscribed within, can be applied to every aspect of the readers' life as you strive for ministry excellence. Bishop Daniels speaks, not as a spectator, but as a skillful practitioner. Whether church planting, educational complexes, or low income and senior housing, effective leadership has been personified through the life of this exceptional leader. What he writes is refreshing, revitalizing, and relevant; it has been woven into the fabric of many.

Personal evaluations aid the reader in envisioning their own life-transforming journey as they develop into the type of adaptive and progressive leader that churches need in today's rapidly changing world You have now embraced this divinely inspired manuscript; prepare to be enlightened enthused, and empowered as you digest new strategies to effectively fulfill the Great Commission.

Superintendent Walter L. Fields, Jr., M. S.
St. Paul Church of God In Christ

"Diplomatic, Savvy, Family-Oriented, Intellectual, Cultured, Pragmatic, Tangible, Strategic, Determined, Eloquent, Wordsmith, Goal-focused, God-fearing, Shepherd, Visionary and certainly Hospitable are just some of the adjectives, just as I discovered, others may also become familiar with, when either making the acquaintance of or under the tutelage of Bishop Sedgwick Daniels. It was a rewarding yet challenging experience playing a role, or I should say multiple roles, in the continuing work of multitudinous parachurch or faith-based organizations founded by establishmentarian, Bishop Daniels. Before leaving the Holy Redeemer complex/campus, one thing you will definitely learn is how to multi-task and be cross-trained to competently handle any task at hand! My tasks while briefly serving as a post-graduate intern were inclusive but not limited to collaborating with a team working assiduously to design state approved programmatic guidelines, meeting site state inspection codes, and meticulously cosmetically preparing a building for state licensing for Youth Residential Care Services.

After beginning full-time employment with the HR Educational Complex, various duties and roles were assigned to me over the course of three years. These tasks included, but were not limited to, assisting with deployment assignments at the MKDC dormitory, teaching assignments at all three fully accredited schools namely, the Holy Redeemer Christian Academy, YCWHC, and the Kathryn T. Daniels Charter School. An accomplishment I am proud to have taken part in was a hand-picked team where I helped to launch and successfully operate the first HR Adult Pre-Collegiate program, fully state accredited. Here my job included Administration roles, teaching, coaching and helping adults (ages ranging from 20-70) graduate with their high school diploma. These various roles gave me first-hand experience at what it means to practice ministry within and outside of the church walls. In addition to the various roles I've worked within the HR Educational Complex, I participated on multiple special events planning committees as a member or committee chair, leadership trainings, and ministry leadership involvement at the local, district and jurisdictional levels. These are some real life illustrative examples of launching out into the deep."

Evangelist Trelanie Johnson-Willis, M.Div.
Miami Florida (Former Holy Redeemer Intern)

It gives me joy to write this message for one of the greatest leaders, Bishop Sedgwick Daniels. He is a phenomenal person as a leader and a Game Changer for the next generation of religious and community leaders. He sets standards and establishes high expectations for contemporary leaders that aspire to become spiritual transformers. During my graduate studies at the Interdenominational Theological Center, I had the opportunity to be one of Bishop Daniels' Interns and the ministry truly changed my life forever. I will forever be grateful to God for this wonderful and blessed experience.

Under his leadership I have had the opportunity to grow as a spiritual leader. This book is a MUST read and is not for the complacent or for the comfortable. It will show you the test and trials of a ministry and walk you through the hope that in knowing that God will stand with you all the way. So many of us say we want to move our ministries out of the walls of the church, however as you read this book you can see firsthand how God spoke to such an impressive leader as Bishop Daniels to do just that.

His insight and influence has positivity affected generations. Bishop Daniels brings a beacon of hope to the young ministers and has served the Holy Redeemer Church with excellence. This book chronicles the very best of what he has learned.

Elder Damon M. Ray, M.Div.
Dean of Christian Education
Wisconsin First Jurisdiction

An Uncompromising Journey of a Contemporary Congregation
By Bishop Sedgwick Daniels

Published by Chronicle Publishing, LLC
6933 West Brown Deer Road
Milwaukee, Wisconsin 53223

This book or parts thereof may not be reproduced in any form, stored in a retrieval system or transmitted in any form by any means – electronic, mechanical, photocopy, recording or otherwise – without prior written permission of the publisher, except as provided by
United States of America copyright law.

Unless otherwise noted, all Scripture quotations are from
King James Version of the Bible

Layout Design: Damon M. Ray

Editor: Alton Townsel

Cover Design: Daniel Taylor, Taylor'D Image Creative Agency

Copyright © 2016 by Bishop Sedgwick Daniels
All rights reserved

ISBN-13: 978-0692800911
ISBN-10: 0692800913

Library of Congress Control Number: 2016918053
Chronicle Publishing, LLC, Milwaukee, Wisconsin

Printed in the United States of America

For More Information
Holy Redeemer Institutional Church Of God In Christ
3500 West Mother Daniels Way
Milwaukee, Wisconsin 53209
www.hrcogic.org

CONTENTS

Meet the Bishop i

Acknowledgement vi

Preface 1

Chapter 1 Biblical Mandate and Commission 3

Chapter 2 Vision Conceptualization 11

Chapter 3 Tangible and Intangible Composition 20

Chapter 4 Embryonic Development of
Unchartered Collaborations 28

Chapter 5 Strategic Programming
and Ministry Implementation 36

Chapter 6 Fiduciary Forecasting
and Fiscal Management 44

Summation 78

Meet the Bishop

Bishop Sedgwick Daniels was born in Milwaukee, Wisconsin to the late John and Kathryn Daniels. He currently serves as the celebrated pastor of Holy Redeemer Institutional Church Of God In Christ, in Milwaukee Wisconsin; and the visionary prelate of Wisconsin First Jurisdiction, serving Wisconsin and Northern Illinois; and elected member of the General Board for the Church Of God In Christ.

His impressive religious vitae encircles more than thirty-five years of spiritual, economical, educational, and societal, empowerment initiatives. In 2001, Bishop Daniels was elevated to the role of Bishop by Bishop Gilbert E. Patterson. Since Bishop Daniels elevation as the prelate for Wisconsin First, the jurisdiction has grown to include more than 105 Church of God in Christ churches.

In 2008 Bishop Daniels was consecrated as a General Board Member in the Church Of God In Christ. In concert with the leadership of Presiding Bishop Charles E. Blake Sr. and the General Board Member colleagues Bishop Daniels has worked cohesively to ensure the success of the Church Of God In Christ while embracing Godly mandates. Locally, Bishop Daniels  focus and quest for ministry excellence afforded the establishment of an urban ministry prototype and progressive leadership for faith-based communities that targets holistic methodologies and sustain progressive outcomes. The schematic of his impact is realized through a plethora of innovative developments, partnerships and collaborations that intentionally overcomes cultural, financial, ecumenical, and familial barriers.

Bishop Daniels and Bishop Roy H. Winbush

Through Bishop Daniels prolific leadership and holistic ministry approach, thousands of individuals are positively im-pacted by the initiatives and resources provide through the Wisconsin First Jurisdiction. Holy Redeemer Houses Jurisdictional Headquarters houses a senior citizen's housing complex, Mason Health Clinic, Holy Redeemer Community Credit Union, COGIC Social Service Agency; Holy Redeemer Christian Academy (kindergarten through eight grades), Young-Coggs University Preparatory Academy (serving middle and high school youth); Kathryn T. Daniels Charter School, Daniels-Mardak Boys and Girls Club, Bishop's Creek

Housing Development, Ford, Owens, Winbush, Porter, and Wilkerson Youth Residency Tower; Saints Heritage Children's Orphanage, Iglehart, Bellamy, Tatum Community Prayer Tower and Rotunda; 20 Heritage Homes (for the homeless and family reunification), Health and fitness center, Hudson-Herron Ministers Institute; and an Educational Consortium for diverse educational advancement all established under the leadership of Bishop Sedgwick Daniels.

Additionally, he incorporates his business acumen and religious insight through diverse board directorships and ecumenical stewardship on more than 15 prestigious organizations and corporations. He was nurtured through his Alabama Baptist and Wisconsin Pentecostal sagacity, by his parents (John and Kathryn Daniels) and grandparents (Reverend General and Inez Townsel and Mrs. Hattie Marshal Daniels).

Although Bishop Daniels successfully addresses many global and community challenges, his contemporaries applaud his Godly humility, enormous personal sacrifice, and motivational philosophy that embodies his testimony which simply affirms to "Have faith in God, for there is nothing too hard for God!".

Bishop Daniels and Minister Louis Farrakhan

Rev. Jesse Jackson and other dignitaries at Opening of MKDCC

Acknowledgement

I am honored and humbled to dedicate this written documentary to the patriarchs and matriarchs who instilled invaluable principles and infinite wisdom into my spiritual being and intellectual mind. Their intimate and personal witness infused a sense of purpose and destiny into my life. Their intergenerational transfer intentionally forged an anointed prototype that commissioned my journey to enhance culture and community.

Bishop Daniels at home church Westside COGIC

The sterling example of my grandparents, Mother Hattie Marshall Daniels, Reverend General T. Townsel, Sr. and Mother Inez Harrison Townsel coupled with the phenomenal familial commitment of my parents, John W. Daniels Sr. and Mother Kathryn Townsel Daniels provided me with the courage to unapologetically ascend courageously to new horizons. The sainted and revered witness of both Baptist and Pentecostal churchmen incorporated a religious sagacity and commitment that ensured positive

John W. Daniels, Sr. and Kathryn T. Daniels

social welfare. Their clarion call mandated community liberation and holistic equality.

I sincerely appreciate the holy bishops, sainted mothers, revered presbyters and committed lay persons who intentionally instilled priceless polities and principles of holiness during my formative years of development. I am eternally grateful for the unfeigned support of my biological and congregational families who enthusiastically embraced the unimaginable vision that I shared. I applaud the exceptional stewardship of the Holy Redeemer's staff and the supportive teamwork of Wisconsin First Jurisdiction. This Holy Redeemer chronicle demonstrates a profound anointing that reveals our gratitude to God and philosophy, "There is nothing too hard for God"

John W. Daniels, Jr, Bishop Sedgwick Daniels, Supervisor Valerie Daniels-Carter and Commissioner Hattie Daniels-Rush

The Bishops Heritage

Mother
Mary Jane Crocroft

Mother
Hattie Daniels

Reverand
G. T. Townsel

Moher
Inez Townsel

Mother
Kathryn Daniels

John W. Daniels, Sr.

GRAND OPENING SERVICE

Of The

Holy Redeemer

Church Of God In Christ

1238 West Atkinson Ave.

Milwaukee, Wisconsin

Sunday - July 20, 1986 - 4 o'clock

THEME: "Courage To Grow"

Dr. Sedgwick Daniels, Pastor

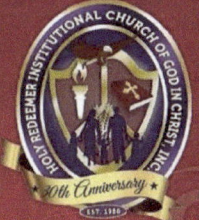

Holy Redeemer Institutional Church Of God In Christ

"Celebrating 30 Years of Ministry"

Holy Redeemer Institutional COGIC

- **1986:** Holy Redeemer Church Of God In Christ was established with only 8 members. A beautiful sanctuary was purchased within 8 weeks of the first service.
- **1987:** A church extension fund was established thereby allowing Holy Redeemer to burn the mortgage of the new church.
- **1988:** A multi-level administrative training center was purchased adjacent to the church.
- **1989:** An institutional ministry was established which included, but was not limited to GED preparation tutoring program, social concerns, and a food pantry. Pastor Daniels was appointed by the Catholic Arch Bishop to the Central City School board (first non catholic appointee).
- **1990:** The first Pentecostal Christian Academy in the state of Wisconsin was established.
- **1991:** Holy Redeemer Bible Institute for adult training in various areas of Christian Education was established.
- **1992:** The first Pentecostal Credit Union in Wisconsin was established. Purchased a 5 acre parcel for institutional and community development. This $3.5 million development would be the site of the Holy Redeemed Institutional Complex that would include a new church building, school, and retirement facility.
- **1993:** Established HR Academy, a partnership school with Milwaukee Public Schools.
- **1995:** Purchased property for the establishment of Dunbar-Blakely House – Domestic violence prevention ministry and shelter.
- **1996:** Established the Educational Possentem and DJ Young Preparatory Academy. Acquired additional property for Senior Citizen's Complex, received numerous grants and tax credits for housing complex.
- **1997:** Ground breaking for HR Housing Inc. and construction of New Worship Center.
- **1998:** Opened Holy Redeemer Housing. Dedication of the New Worship facility, and opened the Milwaukee African American Cultural Center, 'MAAC' banquet center.
- **1999:** Established the Jeffrey Allen Carter Sr. Conference Center for Community Empowerment and Family Reunification.
- **2000:** Purchased a 3 acre parcel for the establishment of the Mother Kathryn Daniels Conference Center which will house a Youth Center, Gymnasium, High School, Natatorium, Retreat Center, Fine Arts Symposium, and Cafetorium.
- **2001:** Purchased 3 additional Heritage homes for Social Services, family rehabilitation, and shelters. Supt. Sedgwick Daniels elevated to Office of Jurisdictional Bishop.

Reginal D. Daniels Educational Facility

2002: Inauguration of Bishop Daniels for First Jurisdiction of Wisconsin.
2003: Construction began for the Mother Kathryn Daniels Conference Center, Presidential visit to Holy Redeemer showcasing our Faith-Based programs as a national prototype, purchased additional land north of Hampton.
2004: Grand opening of Mother Kathryn Daniels Conference Center with celebrity guests Michael Jordan, Rev. Jesse Jackson, acquisition of "The Hamptons" at Bishop's Creek.
2005: Debt Liquidation of Holy Redeemer Sanctuary Complex, ground breaking for construction of "The Hamptons" at Bishop's Creek.
2006/8: Ribbon cutting Brady building, for industrial job training program, and full nautilus fitness Center.
2009: Bishop Daniels elevated to the International office of General Board Member of the COGIC.
2010: Opening dedication of 55 Unit Bishop's Creek Family Housing Complex, ground breaking of Phase I of the Bishop Creek project.
2011: Opening dedication of the Ford, Owens, Winbush, Porter and Wilkerson Tower –"A Pre-Collegiant Dormitory." Townsel, Iglehart, Bellamy, Tatum and COGIC Saints Heritage Prayer Tower and The Saints Heritage Children's COGIC Orphanage.
2012: Renovated and opened the east campus, Old Mount Zion New Jerusalem Church 1527 N. Astor, housed the first student residents in dormitory towers. Started and outreach and evangelism crusaded at Bishop's Creek. Bishop Sedgwick Daniels was re-elected to the Church Of God In Christ, INC, General Board. HRCA's basketball team was awarded as an outstanding athletic department.
2013: Initiated property acquisition and development of assisted living facility. Expanded a health, human services and personal training program, developed a group coaching and male mentoring program, created an educational consortium enhancements curriculum for inner city residents.
2014: Holy Redeemer and Wisconsin First Jurisdiction hosted the International COGIC Bishop's Conference. Presiding Bishop Charles E. Blake and Distinguished members of the General Board dedicated the Holy Redeemer Church Of God In Christ Geriatric Christian Life Center and Urban Family Development Residency. Holy Redeemer Educational Consortium and Wisconsin First Jurisdiction Department of Education established an educational partnership with Marian University, "Trained Pulpit-Trained Pew", which offers accredited Bachelors and Teacher Certification Programs. Holy Redeemer expanded high school graduation opportunities for adults through the Pre-Collegiate Adult Education Program and celebrated 37 adults receiving high school diplomas.
2015: Holy Redeemer's Young Coggs Williams High School became the Division five WIAA (Wisconsin Interscholastic Athletics Association) State Champion. The church and jurisdiction co-hosted the International Women's Convention and Crusade, in Minneapolis Minnesota. HR COGIC Social Services expanded services at the Ford, Owens, Winbush, Porter and Wilkerson Residential Youth Care Center. Holy Redeemer celebrated the elevation of Dr. Valerie Daniels-Carter as Supervisor of Kenya, Africa and graciously hosted the International General Supervisor of Women, Mother Willie Mae Rivers.

Dignitaries at Bishop Daniels Inaugural Banquet

Bishop Blake, Bishop Daniels, Martel Scott, Jr. and Bishop John Bryant

Bishop Daniels with Religious Dignitaries at NBC Studios

General Board of the Church Of God In Christ

Preface

The extraordinary disciple and catechism of my grandparents, Reverend General T. and Inez Townsel coupled with the intellectual astuteness and spiritual foundation of my father, John W. Daniels, Sr. and Dr. Kathryn T. Daniels afforded me exceptional foundational principles. One of the greatest gifts that my mother, the late Supervisor Kathryn T. Daniels, ever gave to my siblings and me was the gift of forward-thinking preparation. Many times my mother would speak in detailed scenarios.

There were times she gathered us not only for family prayer, but for concrete and concise moments that sought to teach us lessons that to others would appear to be far beyond our intellectual grasp at such a young age. We were taught about budgeting, time management, hospitality, stewardship, conflict resolution, critical thinking and higher level problem solving. Mother Daniels used everyday items or situations to teach profound lessons that would stay with us long after her transition. While there were times that our engagement or receptiveness may have been in question, there was no doubt that we took in the lessons that she spoke, but even more, we took in the lessons that she lived before us daily.

Bishop Daniels and Bishop C.D. Owens

As children, growing teens and young adults, we were taught not only to deal with life's opportunities but to ascend victoriously through the valleys of social injustice, inequity and the harsh realities we would face outside of the safe surroundings of our home. As we took long drives to the south to see our extended family in the heart of Alabama, the cruel realities of the nation's cultural shifting became evident as we descended below the Mason-Dixon line.

We were taught to navigate the fine line between, too much eye contact and too little, the appearance of being attentive rather than indifferent and respectful rather than haughty. We saw the signs that differentiated whose mouth could meet streams of water that came from the same well but through different spigots. We learned that as Godly people, we need not fear the law however, we were also instructed to be mindful of our words and movements when pulled over as there were those who held justice in their hands yet had malice their heart.

We heard grown men called "boy" and women being called "girl and gal" when we had only known them respectively as "Mr., Mrs., Brother, Sister, Mother and Aunt". These stark, dark and accepted social mores changed the very scope of my perception about the many lessons that had been taught to me throughout the years. My parents in so many other ways, as stellar models, prepared us for life's storms before they came.

Generally, before a storm comes into a community, there are warning signs that alert the community to take action and then take shelter. People fill sandbags, shutter windows, flood to gas stations and gut the shelves of supermarkets because they are prepared before the first drop of rain ever falls. It is negligent and irresponsible them for leaders to leave people unprepared for what is to come.

Jesus, being the ultimate leader, warned us that trials and tribulations were going to come. In like fashion, when Christ served in his earthly mandates, He made clear that we as the Church Universal had a responsibility to feed the hungry, clothe the naked, visit the sick, tend to widows and orphans and visit the incarcerated.

We were further admonished in Micah to speak up for those who could not speak for themselves and to pursue justice. These mandates do not change in post modernity. In the face of the storms of racism, mass incarceration, educational system failures, predatory lending in both the housing and personal loan markets, we as the church must stand as a lighthouse for those who sojourn through the storms of this life. Their witness introduced us to an Almighty God whose glory, dominion and power is beyond our human ability to contain.

1
Biblical Mandate and Commission

THE OMNIPOTENT, OMNIPRESENT AND OMNISCIENT ALMIGHTY God whose compassion immensely ascends beyond human conceptualization and temporal environments, divinely orchestrated redemptive strategies and empowering disciplines through the atoning sacrifice of His son and the evolution of His church. The unimaginable suffering of Jesus Christ vicariously redeems confessing malefactors and miscreant human beings through a multitudinous series of events at Calvary which sanctifies and enriches God's human creation. This redemptive work of Christ on the cross provides renewal, restoration and revival that revealed the sacred mystery for Christian discipleship and religious stewardship named, the church. Our Holy Redeemer proclaims that upon biblical faith principles, He would build this church and the gates of hell would never

Bishop Daniels host International Bishops Conference Bishop Collin and Bishop Owens

An Uncompromising Journey of a Contemporary Congregation

prevail against it and equip the saints to address sundry issues, while forging a progeny of impressive pugilist. We are commissioned to embrace and ascend the biblical mandates of spiritual awareness, christian stewardship and community service through a global witness that transcends cultures, communities and congregations through the establishment of the church.

Throughout time, the church has been a gathering place for worship and celebration of faith. During times of slavery, the church served as a beacon of hope and inspiration during one of history's most devastating times. As African-American communities in the early 20th century were establishing themselves, the church preceded all other entities in developing a sustainable "foundation" for their community. Through the civil rights struggle, the church served as a community-gathering place to plan a course of survival, seeking solace and making plans for creating a better future for all mankind. Today, churches serve as a place for the community to come together, worship and discuss critical issues. The church promotes family values, education and the importance of serving humanity.

Serving God is the foundation for participation in church. It provides a place for town meetings, social services, political functions, strategic forums, community guidance, community healing, social action, nurturing families, and mentoring the young. Progressive churches create community stability and serves as a beacon of light for our future. It engages music that lifts the spirit through inspirational songs that promote

Bishop Daniels, Bishop Ward, Bishop Blake, Bishop Brooks, Bishop Brown and Bishop Williams

freedom of expression. Contemporary congregations provide diverse forums that cultivate leadership skills and advances opportunities to enhance humanity.

Biblical Mandate and Commission

As urban communities confront contemporary issues, the church stands as a symbol of respect, peace and freedom. Divine intervention, coupled with relevant human strategies, continues to afford today's church an opportunity to effectively thrive and promote programs that results in community stabilization and personal growth. For 30 years, committed Holy Redeemer Institutional Church of God In Christ parishioners have defined a global agenda and delivered stewardship utilizing innovative techniques to address complex issues.

The Holy Redeemer Institutional Church of God In Christ, anchored now at 3500 West Mother Daniels Way, impressively vanguards a community at a complex which encircles powerful worship and a schematic that embodies a planned development incorporating structures that builds lives and service the total community. Holy Redeemer began in the lower level of a former Lutheran School and within eight weeks of existence acquired their first edifice at 1238 West Atkinson Street in Milwaukee, Wisconsin.

As the needs of the community continued to evolved, the cornerstone of that community, Holy Redeemer Church eagerly addressed the sundry and diverse mandates with vigor and purpose. In 1989, various social service programs, youth employment, GED preparation/tutoring, benevolent ministries, support groups and food distribution programs were established and ushered the vision to establish sustainable institutional ministries to proactively address a plethora of community needs.

Also that year, The Holy Redeemer Christian Academy, Wisconsin's first Pentecostal Christian Academy and first Christian school of any major African American denomination was established. Holy Redeemer continued its commitment to Christian education through the development of the Holy Redeemer Bible Institute for adult training. In 1993, the church entered into partnership with the Milwaukee Public Schools through the creation of HR Academy, a partnership school serving Milwaukee's at risk youth population. An additional partnership school for the arts was established with the district namely, "The Educational Possentum". Holy Redeemer established a middle and high school, "Young Coggs Williams High School" and Milwaukee Public School's chartered "The Kathryn T. Daniels University Preparatory Academy" on the campus. This educational consortium was the brainchild and vision of the Bishop but endorsed by various philanthropic contributors, corporations, civic leaders, and a community of supporters who believed in the advancement of youth through urban educational opportunities.

Fostering a commitment to community self-sufficiency, Holy Redeemer established the Holy Redeemer Credit Union, which is the first Wisconsin credit union established by Pentecostals. The commitment to social services continued in 1994 with the Church of God In Christ (COGIC) Social Services. Cogic Social Services (CSS) competed and received several coveted federal and municipal grants that addressed the growing communities' contemporary concerns and equipped individuals with needed resources, professional services and training. The White House Faith Based Initiatives awarded CSS with a three-million-dollar grant to enhance the quality of life for residents in the southern Wisconsin region and provided training, monitoring and the awarding of sub-awards to over 250 community based and religious based organizations. Holy Redeemer established the Dunbar-Blakely House which serves as a domestic violence prevention ministry and shelter. Additional Heritage Homes were acquired to intentionally prevent neighborhood blight, ensure homeownership for community stabilization and afforded potential families the opportunity to embrace the American dream of home ownership. We partnered with state and municipal entities to provide needed awareness and training to obtain mortgages, debt correction, and enhance credit standing to ensure candidates the ability to acquire residential property and ascend from renters to home ownership More than 20 homes within a 3-block radius have been included in this initiative and grants for acquisition from Wheda (Wisconsin Housing and Economic Development Assoc.) and from the City of Milwaukee Home Loan Fund afforded the advancement of this program. Homes were purchased by our housing entity, "Bishop's Creek Development" and restored for adaptive reuse. These properties were either sold to potential families to anchor our neighborhood or rented to families while they engaged in credit modification programs, which would afford them the ability to purchase the home where they were leasing.

Holy Redeemer housing complex initially began with the construction of a three story, twenty-two unit senior housing complex located immediately across from the sanctuary. This project received national recognition by HUD (Housing and Urban Development) in Washington, D.C. as a model project that was successfully completed within budget and proficient. HUD regulated and supervised these and other celebrated projects on the campus. The expansion of housing by these entities includes the construction of a 55 unit, 10-million-dollar housing complex directly south of Holy Redeemer's main campus and apart of the sprawling contiguous schematic of the campus. Additionally, Bishop's Creek, in partnership with CommonBond Community, a Minnesota non-profit housing corporation acquired a 77 unit-housing complex in Milwaukee's northwest corridor which affords low and moderate income families affordable housing. Holy Redeemer continued to advance housing opportunities through the acquisition of an 18-unit apartment complex which has been redeveloped into a geriatric and urban family development housing complex to address the specific needs of seniors and those individuals who are establishing independent living situations or re-entry into society. This housing complex affords employees of the campus affordable housing within the scope of their employment which reduces their cost of living and eliminates transportation cost normally associated with employment.

Holy Redeemer constructed a beautiful worship center. Recognizing a massive community void, Holy Redeemer, in 2000, purchased and renovated a 150,000-square foot abandoned factory adjacent to the church and addressed the familial reunification programs through the development of the Mother Kathryn Daniels Conference Center. This center is named after the matriarch of the Daniels family and celebrated religious leader, Mother Kathryn Daniels, who provided more than 65 years of impressive religious and community service in Wisconsin and Alabama. This facility is also used to ensure core neighborhood services within the Holy Redeemer community and address our densely populated underserved children and youth constituency.

Holy Redeemer is an active and leading congregation within the Wisconsin First Jurisdiction under the direct supervision of Bishop Sedgwick Daniels and the Memphis based Church Of God In Christ, which is the largest predominately African-American denomination globally. More than 6.5 million congregants advance this denomination's global mission to proclaim the tenets and teachings of Jesus Christ. Being overwhelmingly elected to the General Board in 2008 and 2012 was a direct result of the impressive work of Holy Redeemer and Wisconsin First Jurisdiction. The jurisdiction is comprised of more than 80 congregations, hosts annual Leadership Training Summits, provides conferences for Ministers and Laity, Women's Conferences and Retreats, Convocations, District Conventions, and Auxiliary Ministry Conferences. The jurisdiction is celebrated as one of the leading trendsetters within the denomination.

We embrace a philosophy that "There is nothing too hard for God", which has consistently advanced our initiatives. We celebrate the impressive outcomes realized when individuals courageously ascend to new horizons, excel beyond institutional barriers, redefine educational boundaries and eradicate financial barricades. These developments materialized because of public trust, successful outcomes, and the courage to execute innovative and stellar concepts.

Pastor Matthew L. Brown clearly defines ministry like Holy Redeemer and congregations with vision through an edict that has become a boilerplate for contemporary ministries.

> *"Vision conceptualization for ministry is not born of busy church calendars or soleing from church boards, but birthed from the burden of ministry*

needs. *Within the visionary narrative lies a balance of mission and margin. Visionary leaders passionately pursue vision manifestation in real time and real terms answering poignant questions and addressing relevant challenges of their cities. Vision conceptualization constructs a theology as big as the city and provides sustainable benefit to those it impacts. Burden is the key ingredient in the vision process. Vision is the spice and relativistic subjectivity that creates ministry distinction and dynamic tension to address, fulfill and sustain a myriad of contemporary issues within the community. It is imperative that the burden is borne by charismatic leaders called to serve as watchmen for their respective territories.*

The Old Testament prophet Habakkuk is commanded to author a vision in simplicity the courier must not break their foot speed to read and understand it. Vision conceptualization is therefore the business of addressing pervasive challenges which thwart community mobility, economic expansion, educational proficiencies, social justice and spiritual vibrancy. The prophet's vision came from what he beheld. One should consider that visionary conceptualization is extended psychological contemplation, derived from the duress placed on the visionary by their environment.

Many local pastors operate from good ideas and not godly inspirations which stems from the burden in their communities and cities. Ministries should provide direct solutions to imminent problems seeking redress. In fact, one's calling is connected to a specific assignment one has been ordained to address. Vision duplication is not vision conceptualization; Jesus gives Peter keys to unlock multiple authority and multiple strategies for multiple challenges facing generations from housing, government, finances, health, wealth, community, law, society and religion. Vision conceptualization is successful when those so inspired by its ideas make application of its transformative values, thus creating renewal, restoration, regeneration and revival.

What is required of a visionary leader? Visionaries from George Washington to George Washington Carver, to Reverend Dr. Martin Luther King Jr., to Bishop Sedgwick Daniels, to President Barack Obama seem to demonstrate common characteristics of visionary leadership. Such leaders exhibit good communication skills, oral and written. The gift to preside over futuristic ideas, interpret them internally and articulate them publicly and requires the leader to be fully engaged in the possibility of tomorrow. Holy, Social, Scientific or Political discontentment, reflects the disdain for the status quo and the inevitability that whatever brought the organization, ministry, nation or community to these presents, would not be sustainable in the future; thus it demands radical change that causes programmatic and systemic shifts for generations to come. In addition to good communication, a visionary leader should be charismatic and influential to the degree that diverse audiences and resources are attracted to their vision. Charisma that is starkly agitated, produces results from its purpose, not its function. People tend to buy why you do a thing, not what you do.

Leaders who are enveloped and engulfed by their inspired vision will touch, move and inspire others to see, speak and demonstrate the vision with equal passion as the vision caster. It is the charisma of the leader which enrolls the inspired listener to become a vision communicator, vision clarifier or vision cultivator. This charisma also enlists others to own the vision by carrying its weight in communicating to others its validity. Also by clarifying for diverse audiences its universality and application enlists those additional forces to cultivate the vision with appropriate resources.

The leader must be a keen organizer. Administrating vision can only take place after the organizer-in-chief has set in motion the major tenets and operational flow through charismatic transmission of the vision to gatekeepers who will adhere to its construction. Administration is a process by which one manages or assumes oversight to produce the vision. However, administering a vision without the visionary being knee-high in the inception water, will result in altered vision and fail in its results because its conceptualization was changed. Pastors often make the mistake of handing off a vision before it is fully formed, focused and formidable in the hearts and minds of those entrusted with its daily care.

Visionaries are required to be measured risk takers. These risks are in proportion to the vision and begin in small initiatives. Evaluating the risk-reward evidence is incumbent upon them to build the morale and confidence of the team by being an out of the norm or out of the box thinker, who is willing to risk face for mission. The mission of transformation requires calculated initiatives that cause the visionary to trust the chaos of the process and stand on the conviction of the vision anchored in faith, obedience and developed in crucibles. Noted leaders like Washington, King, Carver, Daniels and Obama, *cover the spectrum of risk taking based upon overcoming the unimaginable and unpredictable through uncompromising vision and unchartered collaborations.*

In addition to communication, charisma, organization and risk taking, a visionary must be a critical thinker. Strategic thinking is understanding the vision and requires room to develop and mature. In so doing, visionaries should display mental bandwidth which build operational platforms for the vision to extend into multiple systems, cultures and disciplines, in order to accomplish its purposeful genesis.

Visionary conceptualization necessitates a transformational leader who is focused on team-building, motivation, and collaboration, while maximizing opportunities to elevate the team, organization, ministry, community or corporation to its next performance level. Transactional leaders are most effective in "keeping the trains running on schedule" but not peering into the future where no train tracks exist. One's vision must burden them until its manifestation is a mandate, not an option.

One example of visionary conceptualization which required the aforementioned leadership skills and Empowerment is example of LeBron James and the Cleveland Cavilers Basketball Team. One talented leader laden with the burden of championship failure, filled with discontentment; left his team to move to a championship team to learn how to win. His return to his hometown team after his success elsewhere, provided visionary context for him to inspire his city to believe they could be champions again. His burden was not for himself, his teammates or his organization, his burden was for his city. When our burden is larger than our personal benefit, and our vision is larger than our range of influence, then and only then will possibilities out of the impossible, become probable and achievable.

Where there is no burden...for vision...the people perish."

Contributed By Pastor Matthew L. Brown

2
VISION CONCEPTUALIZATION

THE ABILITY TO SEE THE UNIMAGINABLE requires spiritual insight, creative cognitive imagery and unfeigned faith that courageously embraces an unseen potential in an organized concerted effort to creatively make that vision a reality. Precipitately executing a vision's veracity prior to implementing prayerful strategies diminishes the positive and progressive evolution of triumphant outcomes and execrably increases challenges, concentrations and calamities. The scriptures instruct that the vision must be plainly written to inspire others to embrace it and run with vigor to execute the divine edict entrusted to visionaries. Vision does not incorporate the sojourn or strategies, but reveals potentials and possibilities that are birthed in seclusion with the Almighty during an intentional segregation from personal agendas or public postures. God's revelation encroaches our norm and finite abilities, influencing an intangible and tangible investigation of potential methodologies that will bring to fruition an inspired vision. Supernatural motivation forges an unexplainable quest to accomplish a divine edict, while human limitations exposes the realities of exploring unchartered territories. Inspiration can be motivated by a series of unrelated experiences or occurrences that reinforces the urgency to please God, vanguard the mission's integrity and fulfill the assignment emerges. Contentment occurs when the objectives of the mission are accomplished and the benefits of the challenges are evident.

Holy Redeemer's Seven Core Foundational Tenets:

- The Sojourn of Evangelism
- The Educational Consortium's Journey
- The Fiduciary Impact
- The Holistic Health Initiative

An Uncompromising Journey of a Contemporary Congregation

- The Social Service Agenda

- The Youth Service Mission

- The Housing Element

The holy writ declares and discloses that where there is the absence of vision, people perish and demonstrates that unswerving and uncompromising adherence to prophetic insight which enables righteous populaces to experience triumphant and holistic

Holy Redeemer Institutional Church Of God In Christ

transformation. The inaugurating and initiating of potentially empowering visionary schematics encircles a plethora of skill sets. These ingredients require discernment of resources, astute awareness of environment, perception of barriers, intuitive aptitudes and spiritual acumen that envelope positive outcomes and predicts diverse obstacles to unchartered territories. The amalgamation of a spiritual manifestation and intellectual interruption integrates and incorporates the foundational tenets that embeds vision, conceptualization and infuses the synergy that establishes the structural framework for divinely inspired realities.

Holy Redeemer Institutional Church of God In Christ was established in May of 1986 with eight parishioners. Its parishioners enjoyed humbled beginnings through meaningful worship and insightful

Original temporary site Walter Memorial Lutheran School

Vision Conceptualization

training opportunities in the lower level of Walter Memorial Lutheran School (3205 North 40th Street, Milwaukee, Wisconsin). This young congregation rapidly outgrew their temporary location and aggressively pursued a permanent sanctuary at 1238 West Atkinson Avenue (Milwaukee, WI) within (8) weeks of their inception. Their beautiful and first permanent worship center was historic for congregations in Wisconsin in respect to their organizational date and building acquisition timeline. Generally, predominantly African- American urban congregations require years of existence, financial accomplishments, and an impressive ministry portfolio prior to financial institutions offering resources or assistance. This trend-setting and progressive advancement became a great inspiration to this congregation, their supporters and community.

Permanently etched within the chronicles of our sojourn was the promenade from our garden level temporary place of worship to our first permanent home. Precious memories and lasting impressions are often celebrated through significant accomplishments, historic milestones, phenomenal experiences, astonishing incidents or extraordinary life occurrences that positively and perpetually impact one's reasoning, judgment, opinion, and value system. These treasured irreplaceable moments etch a profound

First Church Home 1238 W. Atkinson

sense of appreciation for people, concepts, dates, and places encircling the glorious event and engenders an inspirational chronological memoir of that sensational occasion. The sage words, distinctive voices, exuberant mannerism, and immeasurable dynamism that vivaciously intensified the occasion are joyfully categorized for reminiscence and approbation.

Parade from Hampton site from Atkinson Ave

An Uncompromising Journey of a Contemporary Congregation

I clearly remember a warm spring Sunday afternoon in May of 1986, when the previous night's trenching deluge yielded to the beaming rays of a brilliant sunshine, as we prepared to motorcade and march for the grand opening of our new sanctuary in Milwaukee, Wisconsin.

The atmospheric climate was exceptional for the event, the synergy and synchronization of our congregants surpassed any tangible element that could possibly diminish the cause to celebrate. The antiquated two-story brick elementary school that had housed our newly formed congregation for the past eight weeks was populated with committed charter members, who eagerly anticipated our exodus from this temporary tabernacle, while hundreds of supporters within our community enthusiastically awaited our arrival at our newly acquired edifice. The excitement intensified through the elucidatory eloquence of our altruistic matriarch, Mother Kathryn Daniels, who engaged the congregant in jubilant hymns, which echoed throughout the surrounding community attracting inquisitive neighbors to observe the massive conclave of saints, the assemblage of police escorts, and the converging of participants and vehicles in an orderly fashion. Subsequent to the inspirational singing, powerful accolades that reminded the group of God's choice blessings and divine mandate to ascend to new horizons delivered by the pastor. The congregation's concentration was focused on the triumphant sojourn and the anticipated celebration which would be realized upon the arrival at the new church. As people thronged the peripheral of both locations, uniformed officers successfully escorted those gathered at the genesis of the journey to our final destination.

Additionally, this promenade publicly demonstrated the solidarity of a committed urban congregation, the appreciation of a worship center where countless community residents would embrace personal renewal, the visionary leadership that would advance community stabilization, and the accomplishment of dedicated stewards who desired to impart legacy into future generations. This passage through our community required media to focus on empowering activities

Parade from Atkinson lead by Deacon Jeffery Carter

Vision Conceptualization

within an economically deprived area and commanded positive conversation in the continued dialogue that debates the significance of the black church. After massive chants, blowing of automobile horns, resounding cheers, countless tears of joy, and the inclusion of non-related residents who voluntarily joined the promenade because of their excitement to witness celebration, the multitude gathered on the parking lot of Holy Angles Catholic church for the final one block march to cut the ribbon at Holy Redeemer Church. The crowd understood that this miracle was realized within eight weeks of the church's initial worship experience and began to chant "one, two, three, in eight weeks (1-2-3 in 8 weeks)," which celebrated the impressive advancement of the congregation, while citing the new address of the church, namely 1238 West Atkinson Avenue. Leading the processional with the Pastor was the jurisdictional bishop, Bishop Denise Flakes, Supervisor Kathryn Daniels, saintly church mothers, dedicated deacons, fervent departmental leaders, County Supervisor Terrence Pitts, Alderman Marvin Pratt, various religious and civic leaders and a massive group of astonished celebrants, with the church's angel choir at the orifice of the processional.

In concert with the promenade were children and angel choir girls in their beautiful array of princess dresses and boys wearing neatly pressed white shirts accented by assorted bowties. The titivated audience gracefully dressed for the occasion which captured the attention of those on porches who began to witness the parading of celebrants. The culmination of this picturesque processional concluded at the portals of the beautiful chapel acquired by the congregation which was infused with fragrant floral décors, red and gold ribbons and memorabilia that was tastefully and meticulously displayed throughout the edifice. The aroma of delicious southern fried cuisines escaped from the confines of the church kitchen and filled the air with a sense of a long anticipated festival. Yet, an amazing chronicle of events that preceded and succeeded this memorable processional were equally impressive

Ribbon cutting at Hampton Ave Location Bishop Daniels, Bishop Flakes and Marla Hood

and fascinating. The resplendently attire of each auxiliary, ranging from the board of mothers adorned in white to the clerics vetted in their liturgical class B regalia was most impressive. The arousing emotive illustration of our community's accomplishments is perpetual and influenced this congregation to courageously confront the massive complexities that challenged our global mission. The declaration and affirmation to expand Holy Redeemer's horizon was manifested during this event after the sounds from Atkinson Avenue into the worship center created an appreciation for Godly attainment, forced all competing noise from radios or observers to cease and applaud an Almighty God and a faithful people that embraced vision.

Saints in Worship in Holy Redeemer Sanctuary

A direct result of intentional ministry accomplishments, church growth, realistic programming objectives, various financial institutions and philanthropic contributors began to engage in empowering partnership initiatives. Pastoral charisma and pro-active vision caused diverse populations to embrace the reality of Holy Redeemer's enhancing initiatives. Holy Redeemer humbly acknowledges the creation of many Wisconsin's Pentecostal historic firsts, which ultimately encircled a plethora of familial reunification and community empowerment programs. This congregation is celebrated globally and recognized as a prototype throughout America for urban non-profit organization. The conceptualization of trailblazing and empowering strategies afforded Holy Redeemer to establish exceptional educational, societal, economical, familial, spiritual resources, facilities and consortiums.

Although the ministry schematic is extensive and impressive, the evolution of Holy Redeemer's ministries is a direct result of unfeigned divine intervention, profound vision implementation, consistent strategic evaluation, and uninterrupted team sacrifices. Pro-actively pursuing best practices and corporate execution has yielded stellar results.

Vision Conceptualization

Holy Redeemer encircles many empowering ministries that has significantly benefited thousands of recipients and established a religious modus operandi for community based urban congregations and the realization that diverse populations require an array of services to adequately address their sundry needs.

Holy Redeemer's Landscape

The campus comprises more than twenty (20) acres in Milwaukee's northwest community. Housed on this massive campus includes:

1. The Sanctuary
2. Educational Consortium
3. Mother Kathryn Daniels Conference Center for Community Empowerment and Family Reunification
4. Bishop Charles Harrison Mason Health Clinic
5. Holy Redeemer Community Credit Union
6. Holy Redeemer Christian Academy
7. Young Coggs Williams High School
8. TJ's Word Connection with an "A"
9. Daniels-Mardak Boys and Girls Club of Greater Milwaukee
10. COGIC Social Services
11. Pitts and Pitts Religious Resource Library
12. Bishop's Creek Housing Development
13. Fowlkes, Swan, and Bogan Senior Housing Complex
14. Lewis-Hudson Heritage Home
15. Mothers' Heritage Home
16. Alexander, Nash and Henderson Heritage Home
17. Flakes, Lenoir, and Hines Heritage Home
18. Dunbar-Blakely Heritage Home

19. Reginal Daniels Educational Consortium
20. HR Academy, Inc.
21. Kathryn T. Daniels University Preparatory Academy
22. Ford, Winbush, Porter, and Wilkerson Residency Tower
23. The Exchange
24. Jeffrey A. Carter, Sr. Center
25. Holy Redeemer Parish Nursing "Aurora Hospital Comm. Health Program"
26. Bishop's Creek Development, LLC
27. HR Housing, Inc.
28. MERCI Catering
29. HR Green Line Motor Coach and Transportation Service
30. King, Scott and Edwards Cosmetology and Positive Image Center
31. Temple of the Redeemed Health Wellness Fitness Center
32. HR Educational Possentum
33. HR Community Food Pantry
34. The Hamptons at Bishop's Creek
35. Children's Learning Zone
36. Family Life Center
37. Cole-Reddick Hall
38. Lenox, Tucker and Neal Music Symposium
39. COGIC Men's Shelter
40. Wisconsin First Jurisdictional Headquarters

As noted above, the congregation has more than forty ministries and auxiliaries designed to advance the religious mission of the church and enhance the community. An in-depth operational schematic of Holy Redeemer's celebrated

Vision Conceptualization

partnerships intentionally reveals program transparency and excellence in service delivery, revealed through projections, evaluations, and outcomes. A Summation of objectives is clear through Holy Redeemer's vision and mission statement.

An Uncompromising Journey of a Contemporary Congregation

3
Tangible and Intangible Composition

THE TRADITIONAL AMERICAN CHRISTIAN congregation's mission, whether urban or rural embeds three central foundational and functional engagements that focuses on glorifying God, evangelizing global communities and edifying active constituents. These components have yielded exceptional outcomes and historically sustained their organized bodies. The evolution of technology, expansion of knowledge-based innovations, contemporary attitudes, individualized convictions, acceptance of impersonal communication styles, the transformation of religious methodologies and the escalation of competing forces mandates relevant and progressive ministries to rethink and redirect congregational

Bishop Barton, Bishop Daniels and Bishop J.W. Wilkerson

presentations, protocols and practices. The contemporary church must ensure the continuation of our perpetual polities of holiness, effectively articulate our Christian sagacity and preserves the Pentecostal faithful articles of religion celebrated by Christian patriarchal traditions, while intriguing a quest from our new population to joyfully reflect our journey and contemplate spiritual renewal. Meticulous and meaningful strategies must be employed that are visible and internal with an objective to utilize intergenerational transfer of knowledge and potential for continued development and progression.

The partnerships that address the total needs of our community have been celebrated and duplicated there diverse missions accomplished specific outcomes are demonstrated below:

First Students of HRCA on Atkinson with Sis. Carol, Instructor

Holy Redeemer Christian Academy

Our Christian-based elementary educational program (grades K4-8) is dually accredited by Marquette University's Institute for the Transformation of Learning (ITL) and the Wisconsin Independent and Religious School Association (WRISSA) that ensure academic rigor, state of Wisconsin educational compliance and certifies the school's performance. This impressive academy is the first Pentecostal elementary school in Wisconsin and has educated thousands of youth for over twenty-five years. The academy has awarded numerous 1st place national ranking in robotics, student ambassador, Tide scholars, civic engineering, innovation, computer program, STEM quiz bowl, mural designs and recipients of various honors. Students receive intense preparation in technology, differentiated instruction and experiential learning through engagement in an interdisciplinary curriculum. Our cutting edge STEM's program, humanities courses and religious catechism holistically prepare children and youth to compete in global environments. Additionally, our elementary school has a vast amount of academic specified areas that are unique to the development of the whole child. Holy Redeemer Christian Academy has partnerships with first stage children's theater, positive behavior intervention and offers foreign language at all grade levels. The school anticipates the upcoming national certification for tech like a champion.

Young Coggs Williams High School

Bishop Daniels speaks with High School Students

Students in grades 9-12 benefits, from our various educational programs and are afforded the opportunity to attend Wisconsin's oldest Pentecostal and first African-American High School, whose curriculum is designed to prepare them for post-secondary education and career readiness. The integration of technology, liberal-arts studies and well-rounded personalized educational programs provide our students with the foundational tenets needed to enhance and ameliorate scholarly advancement and educational acumen. Those entrusted to our tutelage have witnessed stellar realities through rigorous instruction, diverse field experiences and prodigious exposure that has phenomenally expanded their horizons, perceptions and potentials. The catapult and credible gains of our athletic department resulted in their celebrated recognition as the 2015 Wisconsin Interscholastic Athletic Association- Division Five State Champions. Our school-wide population competed at the Regional and National C-STEM's competition where they were acclaimed Regional and National Champions. The committed faculty ensures that a well-balanced spiritual awareness is incorporated within their educational presentations.

Tangible and Intangible Composition

Holy Redeemer Pre-Collegiate Adult Education Program

The mission of Holy Redeemer is to inclusively afford opportunities to all members of the greater Holy Redeemer community that actuate and accentuate educational initiatives for adult learners. Practicums, direct instruction and, differentiated learning styles, technology driven instruction and various innovative independent course of studies are designed for adults to achieve their high school degree. The utilization of individualized education training plans distinguishes the level of academic concentration and element of course completion necessary to satisfy state standards for graduation. The accredited program has been celebrated by seasoned educators and institutions as a prototype for contemporary and future generations. The core objectives of the academy have been esteemed by enthusiastic graduates who have acclaimed a higher dimension of self-worth and colleges that have accepted these studious graduates into their various academic programs.

Herron-Hudson Minister's Institute

In an effort to adequately and proficiently prepare clerics and missionaries for biblical ministries and congregational deployment, the Herron-Hudson Minister's Institute (HHMI) was established. The HHMI provides in-depth instructions and academic preparation in the fields of theology, public speaking, language arts, social work and religious leadership. Students are challenged to define their scope of ministry impact, appreciate the sojourn of the patriarch and matriarch, comprehend ministry conceptualization, defend Pentecostal apologetics, understand exegetical interruption and comprehend effective church management techniques. Upon completion of graduation prerequisites, students become eligible for denominational certification, licensure and ordination, where applicable. The diverse educational composition of our faculty combines seminary trained theologians with certified instructors who challenge our students to incorporate contemporary concepts with validated traditional polities.

Holy Redeemer-Marian University- "Trained Pulpit Trained Pew" Program

As a direct result of an inspired vision for adults seeking post graduate degrees, while attending a Black Enterprise Awards Celebration in Boca Raton Florida, the possibility of establishing an academic partnership was revealed. The beautiful Floridian landscape as it cascaded into the Atlantic Ocean birthed an unexplainable stimulation to transform an array of diverse individuals into a possibility of seasoned adults promenading across a university stage as college graduates. This inspiration compelled Holy Redeemer to pursue highly respected and nationally acclaimed universities to partner with our educational consortium in the creation of an accredited degreed program for working, seasoned adults and clerics. It is the philosophical belief that the pew should not significantly excel the educational astuteness of the priest. Adults who sacrificially aborted their educational aspirations to establish and enhance familial settings prompted the creation of an environment where this previously unforeseen possibility came into fruition. Dr. George Koonce, Jr., Vice-President of Marian University and former NFL Green Bay Packer Lineman and Dr. Stacy Akey, Vice President of Institutional Partnerships rallied the vision with the university's president, Sisters of St. Francis and the Marian University administrative team these individuals conferred through intense confabulations and strategic planning session to chart a course of action and institute an impressively historical partnership with Holy Redeemer. This model was sanctioned by the university's accreditation team and the COGIC episcopacy to publicly offer degrees and certifications. Presiding Bishop Charles E. Blake, during his Wisconsin pilgrimage, applauded the collaboration as "cutting-edge, innovative, historic and exceptional".

Temple of the Redeemed- Michael Miller Health, Wellness and Fitness Center

The congregation's proactive strategy to develop, strengthen and preserve the physical temple during our earthly mission, ensures a greater capacity to effectively serve constituents with a healthy physical presentation. Bodily exercise, balanced nutrition, health education and preventive care measures serve as a catalysts for the implementation of numerous health initiatives. Transforming programs and consistent regiments incorporates recreation, disciple, health information, referrals and adaptive strategies are integrated into achieving a healthy life style. These strategies will circumvent avoidable culturally predisposed conditions. The center has partnered with the nationally acclaimed, "Taking off Pounds Sensibly" (TOPS) initiative. Healthy behaviors, obesity, alcoholism, tobacco, disease prevention and detection are among the areas of concentration addressed at the clinic by health providers in concert with other entities on the Holy Redeemer campus. The fitness center is equipped with treadmills, elliptical, cycles, free and mechanical weights, lymphatic system machines and an array of diverse tools for toning and enhancing body movements. The center offers aerobics, body-toning, balancing exercises, stretching maneuvers and massages that stimulate movement and strengthens muscles. The center is made available at no cost to congregants and members of our surrounding community daily.

Ford, Owens, Winbush, Porter and Wilkerson Tower

Ford, Owens, Winbush, Porter and Wilkerson Tower was named in honor of revered churchmen who dedicated their ministry to the welfare of others. Ford, Owens, Winbush, Porter, and Wilkerson Tower offers 24 hour housing to

homeless children from the age of 12 to 22, serving in the areas of education, counseling, and other behavioral difficulties. This program is a youth initiative that provides housing for students attending Holy Redeemer Christian Academy High School and youth assigned for supervision and custodial care by various governmental and youth service agencies. The Youth Residency addresses an enormous child homelessness reality for Milwaukee County and has 10,000 children under the age of 18 categorized as being homeless *per Milwaukee Public Schools*.

Geriatric Christian Life Center and Urban Family Development Residency

The divine mandate to the church encircles and envelopes a plethora of earthly assignments that empower believers embrace biblical principles and enrich communities. These objectives are realized through the manifestation of enhancing the quality of life initiatives which strategically targets the needs and effectively addresses challenges. The ministry of reconciliation, reunification and renewal are consistently revived throughout the Holy Writ as commandments and commissions. The COGIC Geriatric Christian Life Center and Urban Family Development Residency affords diversity in resolving contemporary and complex housing concerns that impact families through the following scope of services:

An Uncompromising Journey of a Contemporary Congregation

1. The center serves as a housing haven for the elderly and those individuals who currently experience specific life challenges and desire to reside independently within their community without compromising their acquired resources, standard of living, and/or expression of faith.

2. Individuals who require limited oversight or assistance with their private living quarters while inclusive of extended family or support systems residing in house or on grounds in a separate or adjoining living quarter.

3. Residents who desire wrap around services inclusive of meal preparation support systems and/or concierge services on demand.

4. Families that experience sundry temporary housing needs and intervention which could include valet services for those blended families vacationing etc. that desire adults entrusted in their care to have temporary residency and/or while primary caregivers are hospitalized or temporarily away and/or an affordable temporary housing resolutions for extended stay residents on an as needed basis.

The following ancillary supports are also available to our constituents:

Additional Ancillary Amenities

Health and fitness education and suite

On-site Culinary services

Rapid response support services

Unrestricted personal income and revenue

Inter-generational transfer archival (legacy builders)

Organized field experiences

Access to In-kind home health and financial services

Residency plan for total care

The Jeffrey Alan Carter Sports Complex and Gymnasium

The 9,000 square foot gymnasium is a bright, clean sports facility designed to meet multiple recreational demands. It is equipped with dual scoreboards, secure separate entrances, a modern concessions area and spacious locker and shower facilities. Four "sky boxes", overhang the basketball and volleyball courts, can be used for VIP seating. The gym has a 500 bleacher capacity for sporting events and can be reconfigured to hold nearly 1,000 attendees in a stage and floor seating arrangement.

An Uncompromising Journey of a Contemporary Congregation

4
Embryonic Development of Unchartered Collaborations

PROGRESSIVE CONGREGATIONS and engaging communities create cultures that address the necessities of the total person through insightful and innovative initiatives. They appreciate human resources from diverse populations that advances the quality of life and adulate prototypes and outcomes that empower spiritual exultation and secular achievement. These cultures are distinguished and categorically celebrated as progressive. They transcend communities through impressive exploits, exhilarating models and euphoric opportunities that stabilizes neighborhoods and reunify familial environments with inspirational rhapsody. Exploring and engaging compatibly homogenous partnerships with faith-based organizations require intense dialogue, definition of objectives, establishing boundaries, interactive liaisons and delineation of responsibilities. At the level of conception, during the formative stages and throughout the tenure of the partnership, it is important to note that in the agreements, programming opportunities, fiscal expectations and program assessments are vital for seamless operations and positive relations. Faith-based groups must evaluate and comprehend the mission and mannerisms of potential collaborative partners to avoid conflicting agendas

Bishop Daniels and President George W. Bush

and adverse practices that could compromise the organization's core mission or philosophy.

Daniels-Mardak Boys and Girls Club

Since opening in March of 2004, the Daniels-Mardak Boys and Girls club has provided a wide variety of services to its 1,752 members. Daily, during the school week, boys and girls ranging in age from 6 to 18 participate in tutoring, athletic programs, computer training, art instruction, job training, financial planning, Cub Scouts, and movie nights.

In addition, camp activities are provided during the summer months. The members of the club are primarily students of the two schools that exist at the center.

Kathryn T. Daniels University Preparatory Academy

"We must remember that intelligence is not enough. Intelligence plus character- that is the goal of true education. -- Dr. Martin Luther King Jr.

The mission of the Kathryn T. Daniels University Preparatory Academy is to design a rigorous K-8 college preparatory program with highly skilled teachers and an unwavering commitment to utilize the most powerful instructional techniques and methodologies. One of the instructional hallmarks of the Academy is the genuine excitement for teaching and learning shown by teachers, parents, and students. We strongly believe that all students deserve the opportunity to demonstrate excellence and can and will succeed when given optimal support and guidance in a nurturing environment.

Academic excellence and scholastic achievement are an integral part of the Kathryn T. Daniels University Preparatory Academy. The Academy is an innovative, non-profit, public K-8 school serving an urban and diverse student population. We seek to provide a high-quality public education that embraces learning in and through the arts as an integral part of a dynamic learning environment. We are committed to utilizing the most effective instructional techniques and methodologies to embrace 21st century competencies within our classrooms. A key element to ensuring excellent instruction is a rich and rigorous curriculum. Our curriculum progressively increases mastery of skills and concepts in literacy, science, mathematics, the humanities and the artThe mission of the Kathryn T. Daniels University Preparatory Academy is to design a rigorous K-8 college preparatory program with highly skilled teachers and an unwavering commitment to utilize the most powerful instructional techniques and methodologies. One of the instructional hallmarks of the Academy is the genuine excitement for teaching and learning shown by teachers, parents, and students. We strongly believe that all students deserve the opportunity to demonstrate excellence and can and will succeed when given optimal support and guidance in a nurturing environment.

HR Housing

Since 1993, HR Housing, Inc., a construction predecessor of Bishop's Creek Community Development Corporation, began the process of construction, residential housing acquisition, and rehab in the surrounding Northwest side Milwaukee neighborhood. Major construction projects have included a domestic violence shelter, the Holy Redeemer Church of God in Christ Worship Center, a 22 unit senior housing facility, and the acquisition, rehabilitation, and management of dozens of residential properties.

COGIC Social Services

COGIC Social Services is a full service agency that provides direct services to community residents through a food pantry, a nutrition program, family resources information and referral service, youth mentoring, marriage counseling, health education, housing, community development and healthy family workshops. In 2004, it received a capacity-building grant through the Federal Office of Faith-Based Initiatives Compassion Capital Initiative to provide training and technical assistance to almost 400 service provider entities in Southeastern Wisconsin and Northern Illinois.

Embryonic Development of Unchartered Collaborations

Holy Redeemer Community Credit Union

The credit union was organized for the purpose of encouraging thriftiness, promoting savings, and creating a source of credit at a fair and reasonable rate for members. Established in 1993, the credit union is a unique, not-for-profit financial institution.

Bishop's Creek Community Development

The Bishop's Creek Development is an economic incubator for commerce, housing and community service. The Community Development Corporation (CDC) fosters community stabilization and low to moderate income housing at the 10 million dollar Bishop's Creek Housing Complex. The need to address community empowerment is clearly evident through the revelation of the economic factors within the immediate neighborhood of Holy Redeemer. Families and individuals of all ages are served with dignity and respect. For business and program planning purposes it is important to note that the population demographics of the immediate neighborhood, in comparison with the rest of the City of Milwaukee, are relatively female, young, African-American, and low-income.

Within this geographic boundary lives over 13,200 residents. About 45% of the residents are male and 55% are female, whereas in the overall City of Milwaukee that proportion is 48% and 52% respectively.

The ages of household members in Bishop's Creek are fairly evenly distributed across the age ranges, however there a larger proportion of school aged children, at 40%, in comparison with the City of Milwaukee at 32%. Overall, the highest proportion of population occurs in the youth age range of 10-19.

Bishop Daniels Meets with Jurisdictional Leaders

Age Groups	Bishop's Creek		City of Milwaukee	
School Age	**5,269**	**40%**	**192,019**	**32%**
Children 0-9	2,491	19%	98,100	16%
Youth 10-20	2,778	21%	93,919	16%
Family Forming Adults	**4,105**	**31%**	**232,057**	**40%**
21-24	694	5%	51,814	9%
25-34	1,661	13%	94,451	16%
35-44	1,750	13%	85,792	14%
Mature Adults	**2,918**	**22%**	**107,775**	**18%**
45-54	1724	13%	68,351	11%
55-64	1194	9%	39,424	7%
Retirement Age	**997**	**7%**	**65,123**	**11%**
65 and over	997	7%	65,123	11%
Total	**13,289**	**100%**	**596,974**	**100%**

The racial composition of the area is 90% African American and 6% White with 4% of the population claiming other classifications; in the City of Milwaukee the proportions are 37%, 50%, and 12% respectively. In North Milwaukee, the racial composition has changed dramatically since 1985 at which time the proportion of African-American residents was 40%

	Bishop's Creek		Milwaukee	
African-American	11960	90%	37 %	
White	757	6%	50%	
Other classification	572	4%	12%	
Total	13289	100%	100%	

Bishop's Creek Housing Development

Bishop's Creek Community Development Corporation, Holy Redeemer Church of God in Christ affiliate, has been in existence since 2004, and continues a storied legacy of community revitalization. From this previous experience, BCCDC was spawned.

Bishop's Creek Community Development Corporation is a 501c3 non-profit organization functioning as a positive change agent for underserved residents in our northwest side Milwaukee community. We provide tangible solutions that empower our neighbors to live productive, satisfying lives grounded in hope and established through the development of social, economic, and housing opportunities.

Affordable Housing

In collaboration with our development partners, CommonBond Communities; the Bishop's Creek Family Housing Community is a 55-unit family rental development located on a 2.1-acre parcel on the southern end of the mixed-use redevelopment site. Bishop's Creek Family Housing is a newly constructed, four-story building consisting of six one-bedroom, thirty-seven two-bedroom and twelve three-bedroom apartments.

The building incorporates a mix of townhome/flats construction styles with private entrances for larger units on the front of the building and private garden entrances for those on the back which maximizes the feeling of private apartment townhomes within the rental community. The complex includes surface parking as well as a playground and usable green space. The Bishop's Creek Family Housing Development is designed to serve low-income families with an emphasis on large families. Bishop's Creek Family Housing offers both tax credit and market rate units. The tax credit units serve families and individuals earning between 30% and 60% of the area median income. CommonBond's experienced property management division ensures that Bishop's Creek Family Housing provides appropriate amenities and services to the targeted population. Additionally, Bishop's Creek has acquired dozens of single family homes in the area and renovated those homes for families and emergency housing. In 2010, we purchased an 18 unit apartment building facility and also support many employees that prefer to reside in the burgeoning "live, work, play" environment.

HR Academy Inc.

The HR Academy of Business and Global Awareness was a program in partnership with Milwaukee Public Schools Division of Diversified Community Schools, and serves students in grades 9-12. The focus is to provide students with a global perspective as it relates to learning with an emphasis in Business. The 75 students enrolled in this program in 2006 met the statutory definition for special needs education.

Michelle Pitts Speaks to Young Coggs High School Students

Embryonic Development of Unchartered Collaborations

Holy Redeemer Sanctuary Choir

Holy Redeemer Choir Trips

5

Strategic Programming and Ministry Implementation

SUCCESSFUL ORGANIZATIONS become vital and ascend to new dimensions as a direct result of effective planning, competent staff, clear execution of mission, vigorous commitment to established vision, corporate engagement in service delivery and a plethora of innovative strategies. Incorporating and integrating best practices and forging boiler plates to accomplish aspiring projections and the anticipated proforma ensures clear and precise definitions, responsibilities and rationale for collaborative partnerships. Charting obtainable blueprints, designing comprehensible models, composing the core mission directives and establishing benchmarks affords partnerships to exist independently while combining valued resources that benefit their constituencies. Significant phases promote program implementation and each dimension envelopes critical ingredients to justify and achieve organizational objectives. Holy Redeemer actively explores opportunities and deploys measures to accomplish program objects. Our detailed planned development connects our core mission and biblical mandate with innovative collaborative that expands Holy Redeemers Mission.

Mother Kathryn Daniels Conference Center

The Mother Kathryn Daniels Conference Center hosts a variety of programs and services; some are offered collaboratively with partnering organizations and others developed by the center. These programs are designed around five primary impact areas: financial literacy, arts enrichment, culinary arts/nutritional guidance, youth/workforce development and adult recreation and fitness. Outcomes for individuals participating in these programs positively influence the quality of life in the community and revitalizes the neighborhood.

Mother Daniels

The purpose of the Mother Kathryn Daniels Conference Center is a hub for community and faith-based organizations that builds cohesion within a community. The center restores families and societies from factors that threaten the quality of life.

The center continually strives to manifest the Holy Redeemer vision: "One life breached can be one life reached." The community is greater than the sum of its parts and the MKDCC seeks to be an integral extension of the community as a "life construction company."

The Mission of the Mother Kathryn Daniels Conference Center is to empower individuals and families in pursuing educational, recreational, technological, artistic, financial management and spiritual development opportunities that embody the values of self-determination, discipline, character and independence. The concept of financial literacy as part of the Center's mission is designed to be a broad look at how to empower people to reco

Bishop Council at MKDCC

connection, the activities included in this program are designed to rehabilitate financial opportunities, explore new ones and to eventually build wealth in the long term. The components of the financial literacy program deal with a number of issues that affect low income residents around the MKDCC target area. These include but are not limited to:

An Uncompromising Journey of a Contemporary Congregation

- Homeownership
- Credit rehabilitation
- IRA, pension and profit sharing plans
- Investment clubs
- Real Estate
- Earned Income
- Prevention of Predatory Activities (in conjunction with homeownership)
- Automobile loans

MKDCC was able to collaborate with NACA (Neighborhood Assistance Corporation of America) to offer a series of home buyer workshops to the community. During this process, both the NACA and Consumer Credit Counseling of Greater Milwaukee (CCCGM) provided information sessions that educated the immediate neighborhood on how to become a homeowner, budgeting, obtaining good credit, mortgages, rehab financing, closings and down payment.

Bishop Daniels, International Supervisor of Women Mother Rivers and Mother B.J. Thomas

In addition, the community was made aware of financial opportunities e.g. lenders/ lending organizations (including banks, credit unions or alternative institutions) that could provide loans to low-income individuals.

In collaboration with Asset Builders, the MKDCC was able to launch its first investment club. The Investment Group is open to the public and serves as a tangible means to educate individuals on investing and wealth building strategies. Members have been introduced to various financial strategies including stock analysis, purchasing stock and measures yield return on investments.

Wisconsin First Jurisdictional Headquarters

The Jurisdictional Suites offers an amazing resource library for Clerics and Missionaries, individualized cubicles for independent course of study and administrative offices to ensure seamless operation of the Jurisdiction. This quadrant showcases the Rosa Parks autographed birthday celebration and provides beautiful hospitality suites for guest lecturers and out of state visitors.

Fowlkes, Swan, and Bogan Senior Housing Complex

Through the Holy Redeemer Housing Development Corporation a senior housing facility was built on North 35th Street, along with building of a new Holy Redeemer worship center at a neighboring property. The senior housing facility was a multi-million dollar project in collaboration with the Wisconsin Housing and Economic Development Authority. It represents an innovative and strategic housing need for our most valued and honored citizens- our senior population. All rooms are constructed to meet the unique needs of senior citizens and is just a stone's throw from the Church. We also provide van service and other programs that assist our seniors in having a comfortable life as well as intergenerational support from family, friends, and church congregants.

HR Educational Consortium

The mission of the schools of the Holy Redeemer Educational Consortium is to provide the educational foundation that will enhance its student's future academic success and encourage productive citizenship through the cooperative efforts of the Christian community, families, and staff. The philosophy of the Academy is that every child has the right and the ability to learn. There are several components to Holy Redeemer's Department of Education: the Holy Redeemer Christian Academy, the Young Coggs Williams High School, Kathryn T. Daniels University Preparatory Academy, the HR Academy of Business and Global Awareness and the HR Educational Possentum for the Arts.

Holy Redeemer Parish Nurse Program

The declining health conditions of urban families, the utilization of hospital emergency rooms and trauma care units as ordinary primary care health facilities and the abysmal observations of health providers who revealed disproportionate quality of preventive care for the disadvantage compelled Holy Redeemer to initiate holistic health care services. The need to forge a schematic that would adequately address nonexistent community resources, transcend empathetic attitudes into productive cogitation and provide space allocation for these services motivated the partnership with Aurora Health Care, a premiere Wisconsin health provider and Holy Redeemer in the establishment of our Parish Nursing Program. The objective of the program allows for the continuation of Jesus' earthly mission of spiritual connectivity and human wholeness through careful strategic planning and implementation of preventative measures that ensure health maintenance and emphasizes preventative treatment for our clients. This ministry is sponsored by the outreach ministry of Holy Redeemer and Aurora Health Services.

C H Mason Health Clinic

But when Jesus heard that, he said until them, "they that be whole need not a physician, but they that are sick". Mt 9:12

The Holy Redeemer community is confronted with alarming statistics that reveals Milwaukee as the most segregated city in America (Reeves, Richard, Echo of Welfare Reform 2016), 20% high school graduation rate, 41% of African-American male incarceration rate, unprecedented and disproportionate denial of housing opportunities and a plethora of devastating community factors created an unhealthy communities. The absence of a vibrant commerce and thriving familial environments are contributing factors to major health providers engaging in a mass exodus from the metropolitan Milwaukee vicinity.

The absence of neighborhood hospitals proactively inspired Holy Redeemer to establish a community clinic that would address the customary health services for residents. The congregation entered into a partnership with the Franciscan Sisters, St. Michael's Hospital and committed health professionals to provide professional services without regard to the ability of paying for services. Although St. Michael's closed its main hospital facility, Holy Redeemer continues to partner with medical professionals in seamless health maintenance at the clinic named in honor of the founder of the Church of God In Christ, Bishop Charles Harrison Mason.

PATCH

PATCH stands for Parents and their children healing. Patch was established to help address Milwaukee County's strong need for quality programs that monitor and facilitate court ordered supervised visits between parents and their children who are currently in foster care or living with relatives. The PATCH Program offers supervised visitation for Parents and their children. We offer a comfortable atmosphere and a home-like setting for visitation. We identify, teach and offer parenting techniques. Our program offers brothers and sisters in foster homes an opportunity to visit.

TJ's Word Connection with an A Book Store

The Word Connection Book Store posthumously honored dedicated young ladies who were members of Holy Redeemer Institutional Church, Evangelist Terry Johnson and Ms. Asantewa Washington. Their love and dedication to our ministry was exemplified in their passion for spiritual growth was exceptional.

IPAMA

The Institute for the Preservation of African-American Music and Fine Arts in Milwaukee, Wisconsin. We were honored by the Wisconsin pilgrimage of Bishop Charles Blake, where Bishop Sedgwick Daniels is the Establishmentarian/Minister sanctioned this multi-million dollar initiative for historic preservation, educational awareness and economic empowerment. I-PAMA (Institute for Preservation of African-American Music and Arts) project will house the Dr. Mattie Moss-Clark Conservatory, Dr. Roosevelt Daniels Academic Symposium, Maestra Karen Bell Music Rotunda, a musical archive, cultural diversity museum, a gospel eatery and café' and the artist academic extension of the Kathryn T. Daniels University Preparatory Academy (A State of Wisconsin Certified Charter School) and an incubator for artists' in residence.

Strategic Programming and Ministry Implementation

HR C-Stem Team

HR Students at Memphis Grizzlies Game

6
Fiduciary Forecasting and Fiscal Management

UNDERSTANDING THE IMPACT of fiscal management on communities, the absence of fiduciary support for urban communities and intentional redlining that exist throughout American cities has created an economic state of emergency across the nation. Oppressive and reoccurring cycles of poverty, urban plight, industrial abandonment, economic depravations and cultural pecuniary and budgetary miseducation mandated an immediate and pro-active strategy to readdress these social and economic norms which forged the birth of our credit union. The creation of a financial depository owned, operated and managed by our congregants affords our constituents the opportunity to become actively engaged in debt correction, redefined economic forecasting and establish progressive benchmarks in their mission to provide temporal and perpetual sustainability for families and communities. Holy Redeemer gradually incorporated within our congregational blueprint initiatives that would ensure fiscal recovery for the Wisconsin and Northern Illinois communities served by our ministry. Subsequent to the clear reality that our constituencies were subjective to predatory lending, excessive rates of interest on loans and disproportionate disparity in financial considerations was a strong emphasis to our existence. The core and foundational plan encircled customer awareness of personal credit profile scores, budget creation and the creation of a savings plan with contingencies for customary expenses and unexpected crises.

Fiduciary transparency and fiscal integrity unequivocally and significantly impacts an organization's holistic image, public perception, community trust, congregational engagement, institutional depository reliability, civic confidence and stewardship portfolio. It is essential that congregations engage professional fiscal managers and credible accounting personnel that supervise and oversee all dimensions of their finances, budgets, expenditures and fiscal practices. The organization's ledgers, accounts and financials must operate utilizing generally accepted accounting accounts and financials must operate utilizing generally accepted accounting principles (GAAP) to ensure reliability and compliance. When financial institutions consider financial, commitments and various capital ventures are requested credible partners mandate when certain requirement and foundational practices that demonstrate financial portfolios, especially when collaborative considerations and financial depository must commit to funding the organization's mission. Precision and accuracy of records, when reimagining resources with faith-based entitles, must encircle and demonstrate arms-length protocols, auditable financials delineation of unrelated parties from principal transactions and independent auditor's report. This provides excellent assurances to directors, stakeholders, partners and supporters of the organization. Historically, biblical mandates uphold fiscal accountability and faithful stewardship extending from the Old Testament where God required tithing and acceptable sacrifice within the New Testament where Jesus applauded studious and faithful servants who multiplied their gifts and talents.

Holy Redeemer's insightful awareness of the continual and progressive financial needs and options for individuals and entities inspired the convening of numerous congregational seminars, summits and simulations, which provided contextual conclaves and caucuses to inform, instruct and impact effective strategies. These abetting confabulations advanced sustenance to transforming colloquy relative to economic empowerment for those benefitting from Holy Redeemer's leadership. The complexity of the Holy Redeemer's campus, the easily identifiable segregation of entitles and the need for accounting transparency required skillful accountants and staff to accurately discern operational cost and appropriately allocate revenue and expenses to designate parties, while ensuring arm-length transactions, preserving accounting standards and integrity. Seamlessly, the church has preserved impeccable financials that have been scrutinized by external auditors and critical partner which enable financial institutions to commit millions of dollars to the church's initiatives.

Our financial policy manual as created by Valerie Daniels-Carter outlines the principles and best practices to ensure our organization remains in full

Due to the sensitivity regarding the collection and expenditure of money, it is incumbent on Holy Redeemer Institutional Church of God in Christ, Inc. and its affiliates to establish and faithfully implement procedures that are above reproach for handling the Financial Gifts of its members, donors and contributors. It is also necessary for the members to express their obedience to the Lord through their faithful financial support. Accordingly, to ensure transparency and unambiguousness, the Church should follow the suggested relative to the giving and expenditure of its financial resources. The policies and procedures as outlined are biblically aligned through scriptures.

compliance. This chapter will focus on key metrics as outline in our financial procedural manual.

2 Corinthians 9:6-12 But this *I say*, He which soweth sparingly shall reap also sparingly; and he which soweth bountifully shall reap also bountifully.

7 Every man according as he purposeth in his heart, *so let him give*; not grudgingly, or of necessity: for God loveth a cheerful giver.

8 And God *is* able to make all grace abound toward you; that ye, always having all sufficiency in all *things*, may abound to every good work:

9 (As it is written, He hath dispersed abroad; he hath given to the poor: his righteousness remaineth forever.

10 Now he that ministereth seed to the sower both minister bread for *your* food, and multiply your seed sown, and increase the fruits of your righteousness ;)

11 Being enriched in everything to all bountifulness, which causeth through us thanksgiving to God.

12 For the administration of this service not only supplieth the want of the saints, but is abundant also by many thanksgivings unto God;

Proverbs 15:6 In the house of the righteous *is* much treasure: but in the revenues of the wicked is trouble.

Proverbs 15:16 Better *is* little with the fear of the LORD than great treasure and trouble therewith.

Matthew 6:21 For where your treasure is, there will your heart be also.

Matthew 6:24 No man can serve two masters: for either he will hate the one, and love the other; or else he will hold to the one, and despise the other. Ye cannot serve God and mammon.

Luke 16:10 -13 10 He that is faithful in that which is least is faithful also in much: and he that is unjust in the least is unjust also in much. 11 If therefore ye have not been faithful in the unrighteous mammon, who will commit to your trust the true *riches*? 12 And if ye have notbeen faithful in that which is another man's, who shall give you that which is your own?

13 No servant can serve two masters: for either he will hate the one, and love the other; or else he will hold to the one, and despise the other. Ye cannot serve God and mammon.

Acts 8:20 But Peter said unto him, Thy money perish with thee, because thou hast thought that the gift of God may be purchased with money.

(Note 1: The Holy Bible: King James Version)

The guiding principles from these scriptures are design to encompass the following philosophies: (1) our giving to the various ministries of the Church should be done purposefully and regularly; (2) our expenditure of Church funds should be done in a responsible manner and with full disclosure; (3) the purpose of the funds is to support the ministries of the Church, and they should only be used the intended purpose and not be squirreled, but expended with consideration as God blesses us; and (4) the Church's faithful stewardship of these financial resources (both in giving and expending) are evidences of our role as faithful stewards and a ministry / serving institution which has been given the opportunity and responsibility for receiving and using spiritual gifts to advance His kingdom in this world.

An Uncompromising Journey of a Contemporary Congregation

Successful Steps for Department and Auxiliaries

As a department or auxiliary, you are a unit of the church. You are not a sole entity; therefore you must adhere to the policies and practices as ascribed in this document. These basic measurements are required for any department or auxiliary that collects funds affiliated with Holy Redeemer campus. As with any area of the church, <u>there should always be a clear delineation of roles and responsibilities</u>. All leaders must have an ardent commitment to executing and following through.

> 1. The first and most important consideration is to **set the control environment**, that is, to let everyone know, from the top down, that there are policies in place and everyone has to follow the policies. Often, the leader of the department or auxiliary will make exceptions for himself or herself about policies, which sets a sloppy or even unethical tone. Then other people don't think they have to follow procedures, either, and they start cutting corners. The top person can't ask for reimbursement for anything for which they don't have a receipt. Leaders should adhere to policy and yes it is important to retain receipts, operate within approved budget, get prior approval when required and be willing to have your credit cards scrutinized if it is use for ministry purchases. It is key that each leader emphasize the importance of ethics and controls at departmental meetings. Also stress that everyone must follow the rules, all the time. Things work well when policies and procedures are observed. Violation to financial procedures will result in revocation for a department to have departmental and petty cash accounts.

> 2. **Define clearly who is responsible for what**. Every member within a department should be aware of who has what financial authority and

who is responsible for their department finances. All financial reporting should be documented.

- 3. **Physical controls**. Lock it up. If your department has equipment or assets, they should be locked up when not in use. All computers should be password protected. Checks and credit card information should be place in a safe or locked drawer. In case of checking accounts, make sure you have accountability for all check numbers. There are instances where someone comes in and takes checks from the middle of the checkbook. .

- 4. **If there's cash involved** -- such as at a fundraiser or special event -- have two people count all the cash together. Never keep cash at home, in your car or unprotected

- 5. **Reconciling the bank statement** is a very crucial step. It's very unlikely that someone is going to steal from you and run away forever. Reconciling the bank statement means that embezzlement can't go on for very long. Ideally someone other than the bookkeeper/ treasurer of auxiliary/department (or whoever handles the money) reconciles the bank account from an unopened statement. It is recognized that some leaders multi-task, therefore if your department does not have an appointed treasurer; someone else, (such as another member of the department) should receive the unopened bank statement, and look it over before giving it to the leader or the sole administrator.

- 6. Each department, auxiliary and subsidiary must operate within the prescribed and approved budget for your department. If an adjustment is required to your budget it must approved by the CFO.

- ➢ 7. Do not create unauthorized liability to the ministry. There are approved signers for the church and every subsidiary. We have a PO process that must be adhered to at all times. Please understand if you operate outside of policy, then you are agreeing to personally become liable.
- ➢ 8. Always count up the cost first and make sure you don't have hidden cost. You can only expend what you have. If you need assistance with planning for special days or events, see the CFO for suggestions.

- ➢ 9. Do not assess excessive dues to members. Encourage members to work and have fund raisers, but do not over burden people.

- ➢ 10. 4th Sunday is designated as department / auxiliary reporting day. Your department / auxiliary is responsible for its monthly contribution to the ministry. You should also submit your monthly financial report to the CFO.

- ➢ 11. All departments are allowed to have 1 checking and 1 savings account. Accounts should be opened at Holy Redeemer Credit Union.

- ➢ 12. No honorariums should be given to **any person** without approval of the Pastor or CFO from a department of auxiliary. Payment for services must fall within general church payment process.

Fiduciary Forecasting and Fiscal Management

General Operating Procedures and Policy for

Holy Redeemer Institutional Financial Management

We have a fiduciary responsibility to accurately and properly report the financial condition of our organization. Our financial statements tell our story to government, donors, volunteers, and foundations. If the message is not accurate or clear; it is a direct reflection on our ministry and leadership. It also will affect our ability to access grants and other opportunities. Three key components to reflect our financial conductions are:

- The income statement, also known as the statement of activities, reports on the organization's income and expenses for the period.
- The balance sheet, also known as the statement of financial position, describes the organization's assets, liabilities, and net value.
- Cash flow statement reflects the source and uses of cash and assets.

There are other key elements are ratios that we will monitor, but on a monthly

base we will review the above noted documents with the Pastor, our ministry

leaders and finance team.

The board of directors has a fiduciary responsibility to protect and ensure the of the church is being managed in a proper manner. They are ultimately responsible for assuring the resources available to the organization are used as effectively as possible to achieve the results it desires to achieve. The lack of focus and attention to financial matters will cause issues for the ministry. Statistics' report that over half of all frauds are reported from someone connected to the organization who observes something that doesn't look quite right. In addition to the above noted scriptural references for the collection, counting and spending of financial resources Holy Redeemer will be guided by the following basic principles:

> (a) From the time of collection through the process of expenditure of the resources, the Church will implement procedures that require the oversight (physical and fiscal) of at least two members of the Church leadership team.
>
> (b) To protect the integrity of the Church and its leadership, all persons involved in any financial process will faithfully administer their conduct in accordance with this fundamental principal, even when it is inconvenient to do so. There may be a requirement for a background check for individuals handling large sums of cash.

By adhering faithfully to the procedures outlined in this manual, the Church will always be in a proper position to administer its financial resources and to answer any charge of misconduct that may be brought against it.

Luke 16:10 He that is faithful in that which is least is faithful also in much: and he that is unjust in the least is unjust also in much.

While there are many types of financial managers, with varying levels of responsibility, the top financial position in fiduciary management for the church is the Chief Financial Officer (CFO). This individual oversees all financial and accounting functions and formulates and administrates the organization's overall financial plans and policies. They are responsible to ensure adherence to policy for the protection of the ministry.

Financial managers must be creative thinkers who are analytical and good at problem-solving. Accuracy and an aptitude for mathematics and computer technology are also essential.

Candidates for financial management positions need a broad range of skills. In the church environment, it is critical that they are saved and filled with the Holy Ghost and Power (smile). They must be able to oversee cash flow, identify transactional risks, analyze investments, assess the ministry's present and future financial status, and ensure that tax and regulatory requirements are met.

They also need interpersonal skills to manage others and build teamwork, and communication skills to explain complex financial data. These interpersonal skills are critical when they must deal with delicate situations. They must be strong communicators and not easily swayed by the opinion of others. They must understand the financial market place proactively seek best practices. They should remain current on all issues relating to financial management. They should seek outside support when necessary. Computer proficiency is extremely important and managing having procedures to manage online processing is becoming increasingly vital.

1.0 – FINANCE COMMITTEE

A. Committee Membership

According to the Holy Redeemer Church of God In Christ, Inc Constitution and Bylaws, the Finance Committee is a Standing Committee (permanent committee that can only be disbanded by three fourths vote of the Church). The Finance Committee should be selected annually by the Church to include the Chief Financial Officer or Treasurer. The Chief Financial Officer or Treasurer is the Chairman of the Finance Committee, and the Pastor is an ex officio member of the Committee. Also, Key Administrator and Financial Secretary should attend all Finance Committee meetings to assist the Committee as necessary.

B. Duties of the Chief Financial Officer or Treasurer

The Chief Financial Officer or Treasurer has the following duties and responsibilities relating to the financial matters of the Church:

1) He / She will be the chairman of the Support Committee.

2) He / She will ensure that all Church funds are properly expended and accounted in accordance with the Annual Budget(s).

3) He / She will be responsible for the payment of approved items in the Budget(s).

Fiduciary Forecasting and Fiscal Management

4)   He / She will provide itemized reports of the Church's receipts and disbursements at scheduled business meeting.

In general, the Chief Financial Officer or Treasurer will be responsible for oversight and proper working order of the Church's financial systems and procedures.

C. Duties of the Finance Committee

The responsibilities and duties of the Finance Committee can be generally described as serving as the focal point for all financial matters of the Church. Following are the specific duties of this Committee:

1)   Provide annual budget recommendations for the Church prior to the beginning of each fiscal year.

2)   Provide quarterly financial statements to the Church membership.

3)   Review requests for purchase of all items in excess of $500.

4)   Review any request for unbudgeted purchases from other committees, schools, departments or the Church membership.

5)   Conduct an annual audit of the Chief Financial Officer or Treasurer financial statements, which will be preserved as part of the permanent records of the Church.

6)   Review the Church's financial policies and procedures every two years, and provide recommendations for revisions as may be appropriate.

7) Upon approval of an Annual Budget by the Church membership, implement and monitor the Budget throughout the fiscal year.

D. Duties of the Finance Administrator or Director of Accounting and Finance

The Finance Administrator or Director of Accounting and Finance generally is staff personnel appointed by the Pastor and Chief Financial Officer or Treasurer to oversee the daily administration of the Church's financial affairs. This individual will have the following duties:

1) Attend all Finance Committee meetings and be familiar with the Annual Budget and the procedures outlined in this Manual.

2) Serve as an approval point for the expenditure of any non-reoccurring expenses to ensure that the appropriate procedures are being followed.

3) Limited check signing authority in the absence of other approved personnel.

4) Oversee the input of financial data in the Church's computer system.

5) Assist the Finance Committee with preparation of the Annual Budget and associated research into various financial items and systems as may be necessary.

6) Serve as a liaison between the Church Staff and the Finance Committee.

E. Duties of the Financial Secretary

The Financial Secretary will be appointed by the Pastor and Chief Financial Officer or Treasurer, and will have the knowledge and experience necessary to administer the Church's financial systems. The Financial Secretary's duties are generally described as follows:

1) Assist the Chief Financial Officer or Treasurer and Finance Committee in selecting financial software and developing the Church's financial procedures.

2) Be proficient in the use of the financial software through training and continual education.

3) Assist in the development and use of the Church's financial reporting processes.

4) Input financial data into the accounting system for all deposits and expenditures.

5) Maintain records for financial reporting of income (Budget and Designated Giving), expenditures and running balances for all Budget and Designated Giving accounts.

6) Record and maintain meeting minutes for all Finance Committee meetings.

7) Manage and review online processes and procedures.

F. Meetings and Quorum

The Finance Committee will hold quarterly meetings to conduct its regular business in addition to any other special meetings as may be necessary. The Chief Financial Officer or Treasurer, as the Finance Committee Chairman, will schedule the meetings, prepare the meeting agenda, and manage the meeting procedures. A quorum for the transaction of business in all Finance Committee meetings shall consist of at least three members; in the event the Chief Financial Officer or Treasurer is absent from the meetings, he / she will appoint one of the members to serve as Temporary Chairman. All actions taken by the committee will require a unanimous vote and be communicated to CFO in written form within 48 hours of meeting end.

G. Meeting Minutes

Minutes of all Finance Committee meetings will be recorded and sent to all members of the Finance Committee, the Pastor and the Chairman of the Deacons. The minutes and associated attachments will be kept by the Financial Secretary as part of the Church's permanent records.

2.0 – CASH RECEIPTS

A. Church Offerings

For each Sunday service (or special service where an offering is collected), the Deacons assigned to the office of finance and ushers will coordinate in the collection of tithes and offering, the funds will be placed in an offertory basket and transported to the counting area under the supervision of a minimum of 2 deacons and the Public Safety Team. The Chief Financial Officer their appointee and at least one Deacon will verify the count and then transport the locked bank bag to a Church safe, where it will be secured by locking it in the safe, or immediately following service at least 1 deacon, 1 public safety officer and 1 finance team member will transport cash funds for immediate deposits. All check donations will be processed through the bank scanning machine. This procedure will be followed for each service where an offering is collected.

B. Offering Counting Procedures

One of the responsibilities of the Deacons assigned to the finance team is to oversee the handling of offerings and participate in counting teams.

Fiduciary Forecasting and Fiscal Management

The Deacon Counting Teams will consist of at least two deacons. Deacons will be provided the combination numbers for the Church safes, and the Chief Financial Officer or Treasurer will be given access to keys for the bank bags. The counting of the offering will typically be accomplished on Sunday and Wednesday for mid-week collections. Using the safe combinations and lock bag keys, the Counting Team will count the offering using the following general procedures:

1) Obtain the Offering Count Sheet, deposit slip and checking account stamp from the office desk.

2) Maintain lock doors while counting.

3) The Deacon will open the safe; the Chief Financial Officer or assignee will unlock the bank bag and place its contents on the counting table.

4) Sort the offering into the following groups:

    - Envelopes marked for Tithe and Offering

    - Envelopes marked for Designated Gifts

    - Envelopes marked for Annual Gifts

    - Unmarked envelopes

    - Loose checks

    - Loose currency

    - Loose coins

5) Moving sequentially through each sorted group, open all envelopes while making sure that there are no markings on the checks that conflict with the markings on the envelope. (Any conflict should be set aside to be resolved by the Financial Secretary with the Member who gave the offering). All unmarked offerings (no notation on the offering envelope or check) will be counted as general giving.

6) Endorse the back of each check with the deposit stamp. Once the check is processed through the check clearing machine, it should be stamped as processed and sealed in a check security bag.

7) Add the total offering for each sorted group, and note the total on the Offering Count Sheet. Double check the count and the totals.

8) Separate each group of checks based on its categorization and label appropriately. As each sorted group is counted, provide the necessary information (stamped checks, envelopes, etc.) to the Financial Secretary for entry into the accounting system.

9) The Financial Secretary or member of the finance team will (a) enter the offerings into the Member records, and (b) note the deposit amounts in the accounting software into the appropriate accounts.

10) After completing the counting process, place currency and coins into the bank bag. Save the file on the financial computer system and print a copy of the Offering Count Sheet and attach the adding machine tapes to be forwarded to the Financial Secretary.

11) After the Financial Secretary confirms that the accounting system balances with the Offering Count Sheet, complete a deposit form for all currency and coins collected in the Offering and a check transmittal form for processed checks.

12) Transport the locked bank bag to the bank and/or place it in the night deposit. (It should contain all collected offerings and the deposit slip).

On the next business day, the Financial Secretary will; (a) resolve any conflicting offering markings by contacting the Member; and (b) obtain a deposit slip from the Bank for the deposited offering (any discrepancy will be reported to the Chief Financial Officer or Treasurer). Additionally, the Financial Secretary will notify the Chief Financial Officer or Treasurer and Pastor of any designated gifts that do not comply with ministry designated gift policy.

Fiduciary Forecasting and Fiscal Management

C. Other Cash Receipts

Funds received from sources other than its regular offerings; an example is special fund raising activities. For any Church sponsored event, the Funds will be counted by in the same methods as outlined above: The department head or the event coordinator will be given an accountability report of their activity.

Educational and Event coordination of funds are managed in the following manner:

1) The collection and management of all funds will be conducted by at least two people who have the responsibility for coordinating the event; two of the event coordinators will also count the funds using the Offering Count Sheet.

2) Cash amounts in excess of $100 will be deposited in the night deposit box as soon as possible after the event.

3) Checks will be endorsed for deposit with the Church or program account stamp upon collection, or immediately after the event.

4) Un-deposited funds will be placed in a locked Count Sheet will be placed in the locked bank bag, and the original Offering Count Sheet will be placed on the Church office desk.

5) Un-deposited funds will be deposited by the Financial Secretary the next business day.

Payments, donations or offerings received by mail, or given at times other than regular offering times will be counted by the Financial Secretary using the an official Count Sheet, and deposited in the Bank within one business day of receipt.

D. Designated Gifts Policy

Funds received are directed to two basic accounts; the Ministry Budget gifting or Restricted Gifts. For Designated or Restricted Gifts contributions, the following policy has been established:

1) Restricted or Designated Gifts are defined to be any contribution given by a Donor that is noted to be used for a specific purpose (Missions, Building Fund, Education, Endowment, etc...)

2) After a Designated Gift has been accepted by HRC or any of its affiliates, it must be used for the specific purpose noted on the contribution (offering envelope or check memo). It is not allowable to change intent of a gift; the gift must be returned to the Donor in cases where it will not be used for described purposes.

3) HRC encourages its Members to give their tithes to the General Budget so that our basic ministries are funded, and to give special offerings as a Restricted or Designated Gift.

4) The Designated Gift must be directed to ministry items of the Church which are listed as follows:

- Benevolence Fund

- Building Fund or Campus Development

- Capital Campaign Programs

- Children's Department

- Children's Camp

- Educational Expansion

- Educational Support

- Missions

- Kitchen/Meals

Fiduciary Forecasting and Fiscal Management

- Men's Ministry Programming
- Foreign Support
- Residential Programming
- Music Ministry
- Special Love Offering
- Student Ministry Education
- Vacation Bible School
- Women's Ministry Programming
- Youth Department
- Youth Center
- Auxiliaries or Departments approved by Pastor

5) Special Love Offerings will apply to a need or ministry identified and approved by the Church membership that is beyond the capacity of the Benevolence Fund, or other appropriate.

6) Designated Gifts can only be given to the applicable Fund and cannot be used as a "pass-through" method to a specific individual or entity. The Designated Funds will be administered by the Chief Financial Officer or Treasurer (or other appropriate Church officials) to meet identified needs within the Fund category based on an analysis of the need, and the amount available in the specific Fund.

7) Any Designated Gift that is not directed to one of the listed Church ministry items must be reviewed by the Chief Financial Officer or Treasurer. If there is a question, the church officer should contact the donor to ensure proper allocation of funds. A written explanation should be completed to document conversation.

E. Online, Mobile and Credit/Debit Card Giving

In recent years online, mobile and credit/debit card giving has become more and more popular. It is important to have systems in place to monitor and track these donations. It is the policy of Holy Redeemer to reconcile OMCD giving on a weekly basis and track it separately from standard contributions to determine the change of giving ministry patterns. All monies will be assigned under the same categorization of general giving. We must remain and only use vendors that our PCI compliant. All system receiving OMCD gifts must be PCI compliant.

3.0 – CASH DISBURSEMENTS

A. Bank Accounts

The funds of will be kept in the Church's name in FDIC insured bank accounts that earn interest; in certain cases funds may be placed in U.S. Treasury Securities or Money Market accounts. Department may operate a maximum of two bank accounts; one assigned as a Checking account, and the second account assigned for Savings. If more accounts are need, the department leader must request approval. To assist in balancing the Church's accounts, the bank accounts are generally assigned as follows:

Checking Account

- Annual Budget Funds / General Operating Account
- Regularly Used Designated Accounts
    - Benevolence Fund
    - Children's Department
    - Educational Programs

- Independent Missionaries
- Kitchen/Meals
- Men's Fellowship
- Missions
- Special Project and Building Fund
- Music Ministry
- Special Love Offering
- Student Ministry Education
- Women's Ministry
- Youth Department
- Restricted Fund Accounts for ongoing use

Savings Account

- Contingency Fund
- Building Fund (donations by Members designated for Building Fund)

  these funds can only be used for Building purposes.

- Building Fund (Annual Budget Funds given to the Building Fund)

  these funds can be re-allocated by Church vote for other uses.

- Other infrequently used/annual Designated Accounts
- Education
- Axillary / Department Programming

As a matter of policy and prudent management, HRC will sell all securities donated to the Church as soon as possible after they have been surrendered to the Church's name without restrictions, unless it is deemed by the CFO to be securities with high growth potential. In such case, the securities should be reviewed with outside broker on a continuous base in order to maintain worth.

B. Account Signatures

The transfer of all funds and the processing of all checks will require the signatures of two of the following persons:

- Chief Financial Officer or Treasurer

- Chairman of the Deacons

- One designated Deacon

- One designated Finance Committee member

- Minister of Administration

-Pastor

C. Vendor/Bill Payment Process

The bills and invoices of the Church will be paid on a bi- weekly basis in accordance with the following process:

1) Bills will be received by the Financial Secretary or Supervisor of Account' Payable through the mail or other means and immediately entered into the Accounts Payable system, with coding of the expense to the appropriate category and fund. All invoices must be processed in accordance to the Purchase Order

process. Before ordering you must ensure that there is an approved budget category for the order and it is within purchasing guidelines.

2) Where applicable, the bills will be approved by an approved purchaser of the organization who ordered the goods or services reflected on the bill. This approval will be indicated by signing and dating the bill. Any discrepancies regarding the bill will be resolved immediately in a wise and prudent manner.

3) Bills will be paid in accordance with the terms negotiated with the vendor, or stipulated on the bill, unless approved otherwise by the Chief Financial Officer or Treasurer.

4) Each week, the Accounts Payable list will be reviewed by the Chief Financial Officer or Treasurer, or his designee, and instructions will be given to the Financial Secretary as to which bills should be paid.

5) The Payable department will process the checks to pay the bills as noted.

6) The checks will be reviewed by the Chief Financial Officer or Treasurer, or his designee, who will then provide one signature on the checks.

7) A second party from the signature list will then review the checks, and provide a second signature to fully authorize the checks. Unless the check only requires one signature.

D. Reimbursement to Individuals

In order for any individual to be reimbursed for a Church related expense, the following procedure must be followed:

1) The expense must have been previously approved by an appropriate Department Head or Church official, and be available

for expenditure from the Annual Budget or a Designated Gift account.

2) An original receipt must be turned into the Church office, documenting the nature and full amount of the expense. Credit card receipts must also include an original receipt itemizing the materials purchased.

3) Individual reimbursement requests will typically be honored at the time of the next weekly bill payment process, as long as the request is received at least two days prior to the bill payment date.

4) Routine Church expenses should be billed directly to the Church, rather than through an individual to simply the payment process.

4.0 – PAYROLL

The issues identified in this manual address the financial administration of the payroll process; for more pertinent information relating to payroll administration and human resources please refer to the HRC Human Resources Manual. Following are the general guidelines for the payroll process:

1) Payroll for all regular staff employees will be processed each bi-week, typically on Friday. When the regular pay date falls on a holiday, the payroll will typically be processed on the preceding business day.

2) Regular employees will be paid one week in arrears; i.e. payment received on a Friday will be the payroll for the previous week's employment.

3) Pay periods will run from Sunday through Saturday for all hourly employees.

Fiduciary Forecasting and Fiscal Management

4) Time reports for all hourly employees must be completed weekly and approved by the appropriate supervisor before being entered into the payroll system. Overtime must be approved by the Pastor or Chief Financial Officer in advance.

5) Any changes in pay rate, or in position must be submitted on an Employment/Salary Change Request Form.

6) Payment of payroll expenses by direct deposit will be subject to the following guidelines:

   (a) Scheduled payments will be made by direct deposit to the Employee's designated bank account on the normal payroll date.

   (b) Direct deposit payroll option will only be available to Employees who have a consistent payroll amount.

   (c) Changes for the direct deposit will only be made after approved by two.

   (d) The direct deposit option will be provided in accordance with the policies of the sending and receiving banking institutions.

5.0 – MONTHLY BANK RECONCILITATION

Each month all the HRC accounts will be reconciled through the use of the financial software processes. The reconciliation will be performed by an individual designated by the Chief Financial Officer or Treasurer who is qualified to provide these services and is not involved in any other financial procedure of the Church (receipts or disbursements). The bank reconciliation should occur within one week of receipt of the bank statements. A reconciliation report will be created with the original report maintained in the Church files (electronic copies are permissible) and a copy provided to the Chief Financial Officer or Treasurer.

6.0 – FINANCIAL REPORTING

A. Weekly Financial Reports

Each week the following financial reports will be provided to the noted persons:

- Offering totals by major category will be provided each Monday to the Finance Committee via email, by the Financial Secretary

- Annual Budget offering total to the Pastor and Chief Financial Officer.

B. Monthly Reports / Annually

Each month the following financial reports will be provided to the noted persons:

- Financial statement for Annual Budget and Designated Accounts will be provided to department leaders, Pastor and designated personnel. Annually the church membership will be given a full report.

7.0 – AUDITS

A. Interim Audits

During the course of a fiscal year, members of the Finance Committee may conduct surprise mini audits of select accounts. These interim audits will focus on routine accounting procedures such as Offering Counting documentation, check processing procedures, and supporting documentation for expense reimbursements. The results of these mini-audits will be documented and retained in the Church Financial records.

8.0 – BANKING RELATIONSHIPS

To ensure that the Church is receiving reasonable and appropriate banking fees and interest payments for its bank accounts, the Finance Committee (or their designees) should biannually evaluate the services, fees, expenses and interest rates (for interest bearing accounts as well as loan accounts) provided by the current Banking relationship. These services, fees and interest payments will be compared to the services, fees and interest payments offered by other Banks accessible to HRC. If the Church's current banking service does not provide the most favorable terms, the Finance Committee will either negotiate more appropriate service, fees and interest rates with the current Bank or move the Banking relationship to a better service provider (assuming the difference in services, fees and interest rates is deemed material by the Finance Committee).

9.0 – ANNUAL BUDGET

A. General Process

In order to properly plan for its needs and ministries, HRC has chosen to develop and implement an Annual Budget process. The key steps in the process are:

1) The Finance Committee will evaluate the prior year's income and expenses, and will determine the most probable general outlay for the coming budget year.

2) The Church Staff and various Department personnel will evaluate the prior year's expenses in their areas of Ministry, and will develop preliminary estimates for their department, programs, and ministries.

3) The Personnel Committee will provide its recommendations for staff changes and pay increases to the Finance Committee.

4) The Finance Committee will collate the preliminary estimates from the Church Staff, Department personnel, and the Personnel Committee.

5) The Finance Committee will make adjustments as necessary to the estimates to fit within the general Budget outlay.

6) The Finance Committee will prepare a preliminary Budget through its compilation and adjustment of the Staff and Department estimates. The preliminary Budget will be reviewed by the Pastor for his input before the Budget is finalized.

7) Based on input from the Pastor, the Budget will be finalized and presented to the Trustee and Deacon Boards for their approval.

8) After being approved by the Trustee and Deacon Boards it will be presented for Church approval in accordance with the HRC constitution.

B. Fiscal Year

The fiscal year for HRC is from January 1st to December 31st. In order to have the Budget implemented on January 1st, the Budget should be approved each year preferably by October 1st but no later than November 15th.

C. Budget Variances

Any Budget variance that exceeds $1,000 based on a quarterly evaluation of the actual expenses in comparison with the Budget will require further investigation by the Finance Committee to determine if fiscal control actions are necessary. This evaluation process should be documented in the Finance Committee's quarterly meeting minutes.

D. Budget Priorities

When developing the Annual Budget, and during months of reduced income, the Church's general funds will be allocated in the following priority (if necessary, priorities within a category will be determined by the Pastor, CFO and Finance Committee):

- Staff Compensation
- Support Expenses
- Missions
- Programs
- Ministries
- Savings

This prioritization is intended to reflect the order in which major Budget categories are funded both at the annual Budget cycle, and during the monthly Budget allocation process.

10.0 – GENERAL POLICIES

A. Computer System Backup of Financial Records

The Church office network, including the accounting files, is backed up using USB or cloud daily. This will allow both external and internal storage. The USB should be stored in a secure place.

B. Records Retention Policy

The Church will generally follow the retention schedule for accounting records as outlined in IRS guidelines.

C. Merchandising Policy

All fund raising activities intended for the benefit of HRC or any of its ministries, programs, funds, etc. that involves the sale of merchandise shall occur only with the approval of the Pastor or the Finance Committee. A part of this approval process will be to determine the potential tax implications of the merchandise sales, it any. Also we want to ensure the quality of offering to individuals.

D. Contingency Fund

HRC has developed a Contingency Fund that is intended to serve as a cash reserve to cover seasonal income shortfalls and unexpected events that may affect the Church's ability to collect offerings. The goal of this fund is to maintain a balance equal to one month's fixed operating budget. The Finance Committee will determine the Contingency Fund goal as part of the Annual Budget - the goal will be calculated as an average month's fixed expenses from the Annual Budget, after deleting expenses for Programs, Ministries, Missions and Savings. Once the Contingency Fund goal has been reached, the remaining funds will be diverted into other accounts as outlined by the Annual Budget. Use of the Contingency Fund will be limited to payment of Staff and Support expenses during the months when the Church's income falls below its fixed expense needs.

The Contingency Fund is not intended to pay for non-fixed expenses, nor to fund extraordinary purchases; the Contingency Fund is activated only when the Offering Income for a monthly period is less than the Church's fixed operating costs (Staff compensation and Support costs, such as utilities, facilities, etc.)

E. Honorariums

Any individual receiving an honorarium of greater than $600 from Holy Redeemer or any of its entities must properly complete a W-9 form prior to payment. Please make sure their name, address, and social security number is legible. This form must be kept on file for a minimum of 7 years. The stub from the check should be attached to the form with clear delineation of the purpose. If this ongoing expense, you must contact the accounting department to set up an independent vendor profile for reporting. All vendors and contactor should also provide W-9 forms with their EIN information.

F. Benevolence Fund

HRC maintains a Benevolence Fund from the contributions of its membership for the assistance of Members, their families, persons in the community and people needing assistance who are identified through the ministries of the Church. This Fund is intended to provide for unusual and nonpermanent needs. The frequency of assistance to a particular individual or family should not establish a pattern for the Fund to be viewed as a regular source of financial support. Based on the admonition of James 1:27, the Benevolence Fund has established support to widows, the elderly and single parents as the highest priority of the Fund. Additionally, the Benevolence Fund will operate in accordance with the following general rules:

1) All requests for financial assistance must be approved by two persons in a leadership position at HRC (Pastor, CFO, Deacon or assigned Finance Committee members for this purpose).

2) Special offerings received into the Fund should not be earmarked for a specific individual's use. The Fund will be administered as necessary to ensure that gifts are not a means of tax deductible giving to a friend or relative.

3) Funds will not be paid to individuals, but rather the check will be written to respond to the specific need identified. Items that are nonessential to the welfare of the individual/family will not be paid through the Fund.

4) The Benevolence Fund may be used for the purchase of annual Thanksgiving and/or Christmas baskets and meals for needy individuals and families.

5) Members of HRC should inform the Deacons, Pastor or Finance Committee of any need of which they are aware for which no other means of assistance is available. This information should be passed on to the leadership in a confidential manner to avoid problems created if the leadership decides against using the Fund for the identified need.

6) The church will first seek to use government and standard resources to assist in certain cases. At no time is the church mandated to expend fund.

Why Is It Important that we adhere to the above stated Procedures?

Because as a Not for Profit entity Holy Redeemer has certain report requirements. Financial reporting for non-profit entities falls under the guidance of Financial Accounting Standards Board (FASB) Statement 117, *Financial Statements of Not-for-Profit Organizations*. Our accounting department prepares four financial statements in accordance with generally accepted accounting principles for reporting purposes. They are:

Any of our entities that receive over $25,000 is required by the IRS complete Form 990. This information return is filed annually and is due by the 15th day of the 5th month after the fiscal period.. The return, once filed, is open to the public for viewing. So we want to ensure that our information is correct and properly reported.

As good stewards we want to ensure that we are in compliance with all reporting requirements. We must maintain our financial integrity at all times. If at any time you have questions, please use the following rule of thumb:

"Ask and get clarity before proceeding; because ignorance in not a good excuse".

7
Summation

ABETTING CONFABULATIONS advanced sustenance to transforming colloquy relative to economic empowerment for those benefitting from Holy Redeemer's leadership. The complexity of the Holy Redeemer campus, instituting relevant continual education, exploring innovative concepts, comprehending contemporary trends, crucially assessing organizational outcomes, expanding potential capacities and deploying competent resources transforms and transcends the existing congregational mission beyond their current status.

The importation of pro-active strategies and the intensification of best practices, advance the universal appreciation for ministry excellence and admiration for esteemed congregations who vanguard communities and liberate those oppressed. Intense examination of service delivery and assurance of progressive programming diminishes the need for community absolution and emancipates partners to supplement and intensify their involvement. Regularly scheduled examinations and consistent reviews of internal policies, practices and protocols must be inclusive within the overall organizational assessment and evaluation process.

Staff development provides unique and meaningful methods to enhance productivity and ensure professional development for those committed to the perpetual existence of the ministry. The need to provide written documentation affords those currently engaged in ministry a tangible blueprint for excellence and those organizational benefactors who will become recipients of this intergenerational transfer of ideas the ability to embrace a historic appreciation for the sojourners and their journey. The patriarchal documentation establishes pillars for foundational strategies and upholds the biblical mandate of Jesus Christ, who catechized disciples and commanded them to do greater works and expand their horizon.

Summation

The elements of our journey, pillars of faith and structural organizational prototypes have been defined and revealed throughout the pages of this documentary. Visionaries who desire to develop ministries that have prophetic significance and are divinely inspired to motivate mentees must utilize the principles incorporated within the Holy Redeemer model. Adherence to these proven principles afford ministries the ability to duplicate our religious modus operandi and bring transformation to their assigned commission.

The realities of many painful struggles, disheartening disappointments, recurring rejections, and intentional frontal attacks have not been highlighted throughout the delineation of our ministry schematic. In an effort to minimize institutional biases, personal prejudices and contemporary congregational conflicts, the primary focus of this chronicle has been to intentionally magnify and purposefully celebrate the positive outcomes of our sojourn.

It is my prayer that every church planter, lay leader and spiritual transformer will pursue and comprehend one's Godly purpose while employing proven and innovative concepts that brings to fruition God's divine purpose for his people.

Although your chartered course will have moments of frustration, temptations, personal failures and unfulfilled desires, take comfort in knowing that the great conciliator has ordered your steps and will divinely intervene in the execution of your mission. The church and its people belongs to God. We are custodians, navigators, under-shepherds and watchmen who have been chosen to fulfill this will. Inspiration birthed during consecration reveals God's omnipotence and demonstrates his ability to impressively unfold exploits that demands a critical and ungodly society to acknowledge Jehovah's presence, protection and power.

In applauding visible accomplishments, never perceive internally or publicly that your achievements are attributed to your astuteness or academia. But comprehend that every good and perfect gift, appointment, elevation, and anointing comes from above. It is imparted by God's grace and not our works. Vision is inspired by God who embodies an unexplainable philosophical insignia. This labeling carries you through every wilderness and reminds you of his unfeigned faithfulness. Always remember that, "If God can do anything, God can do everything, there is nothing too hard for God."

An Uncompromising Journey of a Contemporary Congregation

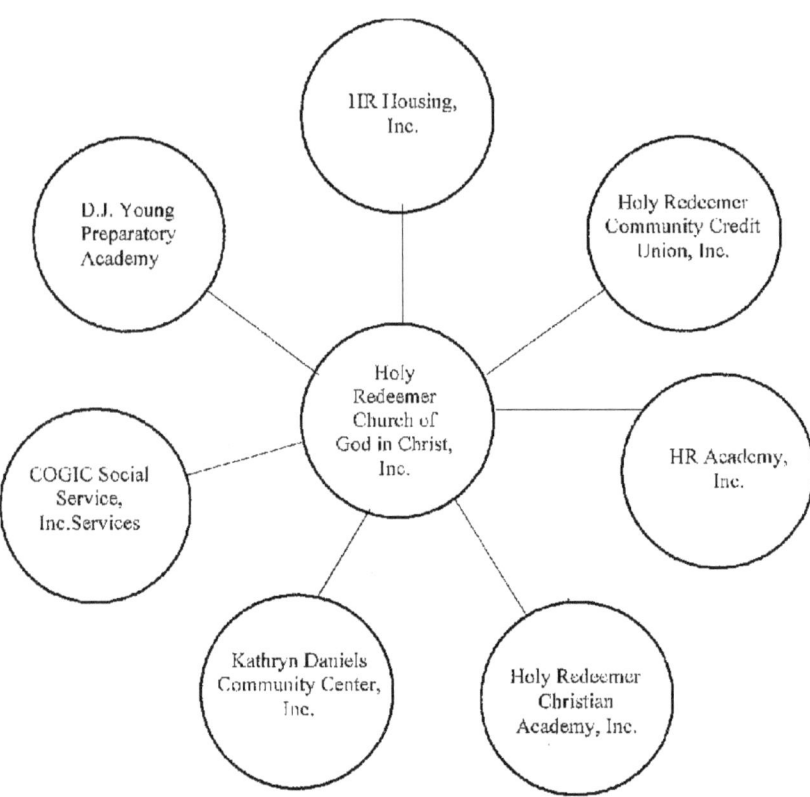

1. Establishment of multiple 501(c)(3)'s.

2. Empowerment by board participation.

3. Separate financial evaluation and auditing.

4. Multiple funding sources based on subject matter.

Young Coggs Prep — a small Milwaukee school with big heart
Featured in Milwaukee Journal Sentinel March 28, 2015
By Erin Richards of the Journal Sentinel

Young Coggs Williams High School 2015 WIAA State Champions

Basketball team puts urban academy on the map Young Coggs Preparatory players celebrate with coach Tim Richert after their Division 5 championship game at the WIAA State Boys Basketball Tournament last Saturday. Young Coggs is a small urban high school at Holy Redeemer Christian Academy.

Bishop Sedgwick Daniels meets with leaders of various grade levels at Holy Redeemer. He is careful about hyping basketball and said the school is focused on academics.

HR Educational Leadership Team

An Uncompromising Journey of a Contemporary Congregation

Tiny Young Coggs part of bigger complex

1. Kathryn T. Daniels University Prep
2. Holy Redeemer Institutional Church
3. Holy Redeemer K-8 school
4. Young Coggs high school
5. Bishop's Creek development

Journal Sentinel

When players from the tiny Christian high school in Milwaukee took the floor in Madison for the final game of the state boys basketball tournament, they were united by a shared mission.

"You're playing for your city, and you're playing for your community," coach Tim Richert repeated to his Eagles team from Young Coggs Preparatory, located in one of the city's roughest north side neighborhoods.

And play they did. Young Coggs won the Division 5 state basketball championship.

What makes that shared mission all the more interesting is how few people in their city had even heard of the school.

Not that it mattered to the boys who took home the trophy.

"You ever won the lottery? That's how I feel right now," senior guard Tiwon Jones said after the game.

Young Coggs is actually the high school at Holy Redeemer Christian Academy, a K-12 private school at N. 35th St. and W. Hampton Ave. The academy enrolls about 500 students, with about 188 in grades nine through 12 making up the high school. Just about every student is African-American and low-income, and attending with the help of a taxpayer-funded tuition subsidy, or voucher.

Most small private schools don't usually offer much in the way of sports programs, but in light of the success at Young Coggs — and students asking for more programs — leaders are now thinking of ways to expand.

"Obviously athletics is going to become a new discussion for us in light of our recent success," said Bishop Sedgwick Daniels, who oversees all the operations at Holy Redeemer and its affiliate operations.

Basketball got the most early traction, and the school hired Richert a few years ago as a physical education teacher who could also coach the boys basketball team.

Richert, 42, cut his teeth with coaching jobs at St. John's Northwestern Military Academy and at a small rural school in Wisconsin before coming to Holy Redeemer. His father had been a high school and college basketball coach —

including a stint at Carroll in Waukesha — where Richert played on the team under his dad's direction.

Only Urban Team

Young Coggs was the only urban school from the central city that made it to the state basketball championships this year, from any of the five divisions. In fact, the Eagles had never even made it past the regional finals before this year.

This year was different. The teammates gathered in a conference room to discuss their victory on a recent morning. They all wore matching red ball caps with the words, "Dreams Never Expire" on the front. A donor had dropped them off.

DeAngelo Crawford, a senior point guard, said it was all about team chemistry.

"We really got to know each other," he said.

"Our friends and family really motivated us to play hard," added Eric Harper, a junior.

None expected the number of lights and cameras and media at the Kohl Center. The regulation-sized court was noticeably bigger than the small court they play on at Holy Reedemer, flanked on one side by four expandable bleachers.

In Madison, the crowd included thousands of people.

Neighborhood Epicenter

Daniels oversees Holy Redeemer Church of God in Christ, the church at the epicenter of a complex that includes Holy Redeemer Academy as well as a K-8 public charter school that's authorized by Milwaukee Public Schools: Kathryn T. Daniels University Preparatory Academy.

There's also housing for children in distress, a credit union, a food pantry, a medical clinic and a property development enterprise called Bishop's Creek Community Development Corp.

Daniels said leaders distinguished the high school at Holy Redeemer with a different name within the past few years to honor well-known black leaders. Young Coggs came from David Johnson Young, a preacher who started a Gospel literature publishing house in Kansas City, and his granddaughter Marcia P. Coggs, a former Wisconsin state representative who died in 2003.

Recently, a third name has been added to the high school. It's now officially known as "Young Coggs Williams," after Annette Polly Williams, the longest-serving woman in the Wisconsin state Legislature and a school choice pioneer. She [died in the fall of 2014](#).

Daniels is careful about hyping basketball and said the school is focused on academic excellence. But because students and donors have asked for more sports opportunities, Daniels said they will likely create volleyball and track teams. And next year, Young Coggs may play high school football with the neighboring Obama School of Career and Technical Education, in the Custer complex.

Daniels recently reminded the players of their status as role models, then rattled off the college visits they'd be going on this spring. Still, many of the Young Coggs players said basketball was one of the main reasons they wanted to come to school. Richert frequently tells them they should use their recent win as their ticket to bigger and better opportunities. "Take this as far as you can," he said.

Summation

African American arts center planned at Bishop's Creek

Non-profit group seeking zoning change to industrial building

by [Corrinne Hess](#)

August 09, 2016, 12:39 PM

A Milwaukee church group is planning to convert an industrial building on the city's far northwest side into an African American arts center.

I-PAMA Pre-Construction

This warehouse could be converted into an African American arts center.

The Bishop's Creek CDC, an affiliate of Holy Redeemer Institutional Church of God in Christ in Milwaukee, has asked the city to change the zoning of 3200 W. Hampton Ave., a one-story warehouse at the northwest corner of West Hampton Avenue and N. 32nd Street.

The group wants to use the space as the Institute for the Preservation of African-American Music and Arts to advance the current educational courses offered by the Holy Redeemer Educational Consortium.

The building will be renovated and used as an e-library, a theater, classrooms for art and other activities, a small museum, café, and offices to support the activities on site, according to plans submitted to the city.

The African American music and arts center development is the latest phase of the Bishop's Creek redevelopment project. The Bishop's Creek redevelopment site was the former Kaiser/Greenbaum Tannery Property at the southwest corner N. 32nd Street and Hampton Avenue on the city's northwest side.

The central portion of the property was occupied by the Greenebaum Tannery from the 1920s to the mid-1950s and housed everything from a paint spray booth to an automotive salvage facility to a machine shop. The Kaiser family operated a business incubator in the locations from the 1950s until 2001.

In 2004, the Bishop's Creek CDC was formed and began working on restoring the property. The site covers an approximately 1.5 square mile area.

In 2008, the city created a $1.6 million tax incremental financing district to pay for building demolition and cleanup of a former tannery.

In 2010, Bishop's Creek Family Housing opened. The 55-unit apartment building at 4765 N. 32nd St., was developed by an affiliate of St. Paul-based developer CommonBond Communities Inc., in partnership with Bishop's Creek Community Development Corp.

Summation

Church to build large community center in central city

"Our purpose and intent is to serve as many residents as we can, so it was to our advantage to acquire (the building). It flows right in to our present location."

— Alvin Inverse,
Holy Redeemer Institutional Church of God in Christ

HR Housing, Inc., the housing-development affiliate of Holy Redeemer Church of God in Christ, built a 22-unit elderly housing project on vacant land adjacent to the church.

Holy Redeemer Church of God in Christ and its nonprofit housing-development affiliate, HR Housing, Inc., constructed a three-story elevator building providing 22 one-bedroom apartments for elderly residents. The building was constructed on vacant land adjacent to facilities operated by the church.

The project is part of a multifaceted effort by Holy Redeemer to provide a range of educational opportunities and support services for members of the church and the surrounding community. The project involved a number of nonprofit organizations and a variety of funding sources in its operations and its financing. HR Housing used the consulting services of the Wisconsin Partnership for Housing Development, a 10-year old nonprofit housing organization. The project is managed by the nonprofit Milwaukee Housing Assistance Corporation, which owns a number of projects in the neighborhood.

Financing for the $1.6 million project came from FHLB member North Milwaukee State Bank, a Section 120 loan from the City of Milwaukee, and a consortium of Milwaukee-based financial institutions and corporations. The project received WHEDA tax credits, and equity was provided by the Housing Equity Fund. North Milwaukee State Bank, which provided construction and permanent financing, used both the AHP and the CIP to support this initiative, providing a $110,000 AHP subsidy and funding the permanent mortgage with a $506,000 CIP advance.

An Uncompromising Journey of a Contemporary Congregation

316 N Milwaukee St, STE 406
Milwaukee, WI 53202-5818
(414) 297-1140

2245 Rayburn Building
Washington, D.C. 20515
(202) 225-4572

May 27, 2016

Bishop Sedgwick Daniels, Sr. Pastor
Holy Redeemer Church of God in Christ
3500 W. Mother Daniels Way
Milwaukee, WI 53209-5311

Dear Bishop Daniels,

It is indeed an honor for me to have this opportunity to express my thanks and acknowledge your 30 years of servant leadership as the pastor of Holy Redeemer Church of God in Christ (COGIC).

Bishop Daniels, there is a scripture in the Bible that says in short, "the greatest are those who serve others." Through your visionary leadership, Holy Redeemer COGIC has endeavored to live out this doctrine daily through the provision of a myriad of services, ministries, and programs to congregants and the broader Milwaukee community. Numerous holistic and life altering services are provided via your ministerial partners and programmatic affiliates to thousands of individuals, families, community constituents, and denominational members. The services include: Spiritual advancement, community development, housing, education, Mother Kathryn Daniels Conference Center, and Bishops Creek, a multi-purpose living facility. Holy Redeemer's national prominence has also been recognized through your elevation to the International Office of General Board Member of the COGIC, as well as Sister Valerie Daniels' elevation as Supervisor of East Kenya, Africa. I thank you so much for your dedication and commitment to the serve "All of God's Children."

Over the past 30 years, Holy Redeemer has been a catalyst for transforming lives and changing the conditions of those residing in Milwaukee's 4th Congressional District. Mother Kathryn Daniels, under whose name and inspiration we gather for today's celebration, would most certainly be proud of all you have accomplished. I join with your congregation, family, community leaders and friends in thanking you for these efforts, and for the many blessings bestowed on Milwaukee by your work.

Sincerely,

Gwen Moore
Member of Congress

GM/rs

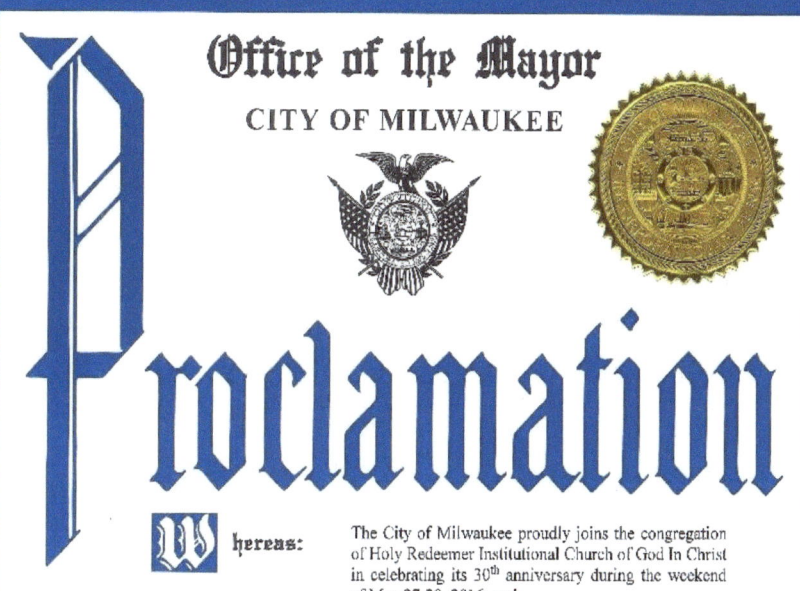

Office of the Mayor
CITY OF MILWAUKEE

Proclamation

Whereas, The City of Milwaukee proudly joins the congregation of Holy Redeemer Institutional Church of God In Christ in celebrating its 30th anniversary during the weekend of May 27-29, 2016; and,

WHEREAS, Holy Redeemer Institutional Church of God In Christ was established in 1986 and has expanded into a multi-purpose complex that houses an administrative training center, an institutional ministry for GED preparation tutoring programs, a food pantry and a social concern resource center; and,

WHEREAS, Holy Redeemer Institutional Church of God In Christ has experienced remarkable growth and development, serving as a catalyst for spiritual and physical growth for its congregation through faith based programs and initiatives; and,

WHEREAS, Holy Redeemer Institutional Church of God In Christ is committed to serving the diverse needs of the greater Milwaukee community through its ministerial services and programs, including MPS partnerships, health and human services programs, property development for family housing complexes and conference and culture centers; and,

WHEREAS, The City of Milwaukee congratulates Holy Redeemer Institutional Church of God In Christ on 30 years of dedicated service and leadership, recognizes its outstanding contributions to the community and wishes it many more years of success;

NOW, THEREFORE, I, TOM BARRETT, Mayor of the City of Milwaukee, do hereby proclaim May 27-29, 2016, to be

HOLY REDEEMER INSTITUTIONAL CHURCH OF GOD IN CHRIST WEEKEND

throughout the City of Milwaukee.

Tom Barrett

TOM BARRETT
Mayor

An Uncompromising Journey of a Contemporary Congregation

TAMMY BALDWIN
UNITED STATES SENATOR

May 2016

Dear Bishop Daniels,

Congratulations on the 30th anniversary of Holy Redeemer Institutional Church of God in Christ! I am delighted to recognize Holy Redeemer for your long-standing commitment to your congregants and to the broader community in the Greater Milwaukee area.

As a congregation determined to be a source of spirituality, faith and service to your community, your message of hope and renewal has flourished. From your humble beginnings as congregation of eight members, your congregation has experienced a tremendous amount of growth and change. Today, in collaboration with your ministerial partners and programmatic affiliates, Holy Redeemer has an impressive record of providing spiritual guidance, as well as life-changing community services and facilities.

You are truly a congregation who has put your faith into action and words into deeds. I am pleased to join others in acknowledging your three decades of service to your neighbors. The work that you do each day in reaching out to individuals of all ages and backgrounds and addressing the needs of the whole person is extraordinary. Thank you for the role that you play in strengthening our families and community.

Again, congratulations on this wonderful milestone. I wish you and your congregation continued success in the years to come.

Sincerely,

Tammy Baldwin
United States Senator

NOT PRINTED AT GOVERNMENT EXPENSE

Executive Proclamation

WHEREAS, Holy Redeemer Institutional Church of God In Christ was established in 1986 with only 8 members and a beautiful sanctuary was purchased within 8 weeks of the first service. A church extension fund was established thereby allowing Holy Redeemer to burn the mortgage of the new church; an

WHEREAS, Holy Redeemer purchased a 3 acre parcel of land for establishment of the Mother Kathryn Daniels Conference Center which houses a youth center, gymnasium, natatorium, retreat Center, fine arts symposium and cafeteria; and

WHEREAS, the celebration of the grand opening of Mother Kathryn Daniels Conference Center was attended by celebrity guests Michael Jordan, the Reverend Jessie Jackson, Yolanda Adams and Kwame Jackson; and

WHEREAS, Holy Redeemer also opened the Brady Building, a site for an industrial training program with a nautilus fitness center; and

WHEREAS, Bishop Daniels was elevated to the international office of General Board Member of the COGIC; and

WHEREAS, Holy Redeemer expanded high school graduation opportunities for adults through the Pre-Collegiate Adult Education Program and celebrated the graduation of 37 adults; and

WHEREAS, Holy Redeemer and Wisconsin First Jurisdiction hosted the International COGIC Bishop's Conference, Presiding Bishop Charles E Blake and Distinguished members of the General Board dedicated the Holy Redeemer Church of GOD in Christ Geriatric Christian Life Center and Urban Family Development Residency; and

WHEREAS, Holy Redeemer celebrated the elevation of Dr. Valerie Daniels-Carter s Supervisor of Kenya, Africa and graciously hosted the International General Supervisor of Women, Mother Willie Mae Rivers; and

WHEREAS, Holy Redeemer Institutional Church of God in Christ has been a source of powerful worship, community engagement and innovative programming and development; now therefore

I, CHRIS ABELE, County Executive of Milwaukee County do hereby commend

Holy Redeemer Institutional Church of God in Christ

for 30 years of excellent service in the Milwaukee Community.

Chris Abele
Milwaukee County Executive

An Uncompromising Journey of a Contemporary Congregation

Summation

Summation

Bishop Blake and General Board assisting Bishop Daniels in the Opening of the GLC

www.ingramcontent.com/pod-product-compliance
Lightning Source LLC
Chambersburg PA
CBHW041614220426
43670CB00001B/16